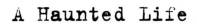

A Haunted Life

Photo By John A. Tarulli

About the Author

Debra Robinson is a professional psychic and carries on a dual career in music as a performer and songwriter.

She works with Haunted Heartland Tours (www. hauntedhistory.net) and as a floating member of several paranormal investigation groups. Debra does private readings and volunteers for various online metaphysical sites. She heads JSMS, an annual charity skating event, and lives in a haunted house in a small town in Ohio.

The True Ghost Story of a
Reluctant Psychic

A Haunted Life

Debra Robinson

Llewellyn Publications
Woodbury, Minnesota

First Edition
First Printing, 2013

Book design by Bob Gaul
Cover design by Gavin Dayton Duffy
Cover images: Woman © iStockphoto.com/Forest Woodward
     Grungy paper © iStockphoto.com/andipantz
     Burned paper © iStockphoto.com/Kim Sohee
Editing by Ed Day
Interior photos of James by Dave DiNuzzo

Llewellyn Publications is a registered trademark of Llewellyn Worldwide Ltd.

Library of Congress Cataloging-in-Publication Data
Robinson, Debra, 1955–
 A haunted life: the true ghost story of a reluctant psychic/Debra Robinson.—
1st ed.
  pages cm.
 ISBN 978-0-7387-3641-9
1. Robinson, Debra, 1955– 2. Women psychics—Biography. I. Title.
 BF1283.R67A3 2013
 133.8092—dc23
 [B]
       2012051684

Llewellyn Publications
A Division of Llewellyn Worldwide Ltd.
2143 Wooddale Drive
Woodbury, MN 55125-2989
www.llewellyn.com

Printed in the United States of America

Contents

Acknowledgments

To my sweet boy James; thank you for who you were. The world's a better place for your having lived. I can only imagine what might have been. I miss you…

Dad: Thank you for the music, and being the best father I could ever have. Until we meet again…

Rod: Thanks for the child we created and loved, all the years of memories, friendship, and loyalty, and for sharing the grief only we can know.

Joyce "Veece": For all you've done, but mostly, for always being there for me.

Special thanks to:

Llewellyn Worldwide, Lisa Allen, editor Amy Glaser; Betsy Robinson, Sandy K., Sherri Brake, Terry Iacuzzo, John Kachuba, J. J. Ong, Toni Dore; and John T., for keeping the music world going for me. I literally couldn't do it without you.

Thanks to James's friends, the skaters who shared his greatest pleasure, his sponsors, and the musicians, for making his short life so happy. Thanks for getting us through that first year, and for helping with the JSMS.

I ask that everyone reading this remember how quickly a life can end, how devastating the loss to all involved, so please, if you're drinking, don't drive.

And last but certainly not least, thanks to God for bringing me through it with gratitude for the gifts He's given me, the greatest one being James.

Foreword

Haunted. To many people, the word conjures up images of dimly lit houses with gaping broken windows, spooky rural roads that twist through darkened woods, creepy cemetery vaults, paranormal oddities, and the unknown. To a few of us who actually make a living in the field of the paranormal, it's just another day because for us, the paranormal…is normal.

As a paranormal investigator, haunted tour owner, and author, I come in contact with people and places that are haunted or have "issues." I've had over twenty-five years of investigating the paranormal and during this time I've met some interesting and intriguing people. Quite a few of the people I've met in my travels have claimed to have gifts of the metaphysical sort and many of these, as expected, have fallen short of an inkling of credibility. Debra Robinson is the real deal and in more ways than just being a psychic.

A Haunted Life: The True Ghost Story of a Reluctant Psychic is a venture into a woman's life that takes you and holds you from the first typed word to the last page turn. Debra Robinson, as the title implies, has been a bit reluctant with regard to her spiritual gifts at times. Debra takes her abilities in stride nowadays, but it wasn't always that simple.

The feedback over the years since our first meeting has been wonderful with respect to Debra's readings for my company. Our friendship grew as did our professional respect for each other. I was blessed to meet her son James when he attended a hunt of mine in West Virginia.

Life is full of ups and downs on this roller coaster called "existence" as we all know. Debra has lived life and experienced it all. As a friend, Debra drew me into her network of family and friends. As a writer, she drew me into her story, as I'm sure she will do for you.

Enjoy the journey.

—Sherri Brake
Author and Paranormal Researcher
Summersville, West Virginia

Introduction

I've never really thought of myself as a writer; I'm a song-writer, a musician—and a psychic. But I was compelled to tell this story. I couldn't tell it without mixing personal with paranormal. I can't separate it. I may not know all the writing "rules," but I know what happened to me, and this is it—this is a true story. It's about a lifelong battle with evil. It's about haunted houses. And it's about psychic abilities.

Most names have been changed. I stand behind the events and hope minor mistakes are forgiven. I only had to shift time in a couple places to speed things up. Also note that my opinions are my own—I don't represent all psychics—and I've chosen to include these thoughts because of the personal nature of this book.

Did you ever feel like purging yourself of all the bad that's happened? Just get it all out and leave it behind?

That's how I'm feeling right now. So bear with me while I purge this scary, strange story. Because I've found truth really is stranger than fiction.

Yes, I said scary—I hope it's scary enough to make you think twice about messing with certain things. It still scares me too. If you believe in a God, you almost always believe in His opposite. I *know* it's there. I've seen it and heard it. I pray you'll take away an understanding of what may happen if you accidently let it in. You really don't want to do that.

Though I've had this strange psychic gift all my life and have helped others, I've rarely been able to help myself. I've heard similar stories from other psychics. Maybe that's part of the curse. But that pales in comparison to another possibility—a possibility that's plagued me for a while: that this life I've led, filled with the supernatural, might have contributed in some way to what's happened.

Is psychic ability good or evil? If it's from God: probably good. If not: probably bad. Supposedly, it's a spiritual gift, but this is what I wrestle with most. Or maybe it's just a physiological condition some are born with. Something that helped the cavemen survive.

I want to start at the beginning; to lay it out for inspection and give others hope that there's more than just this life. But I also want it to be a cautionary tale. I'm a rational person, but I no longer believe in coincidences— I've witnessed too many to conclude otherwise.

I now believe there's an epic cosmic battle between good and evil that plays out every day in the here and now. I believe our daily choices, even seemingly insignificant decisions, are the result of influence by whichever side is winning at that moment. I believe our actions align us either with the "light" or the "dark." And that pesky free will thing makes us responsible for our choices. Until recently, I believed rain would fall on the just and the unjust; no one escaped it. Only lately have I felt there's a little more going on here.

Do we sometimes take on more responsibility for the way things turn out than we're aware of? I have my suspicions. But I'll let you decide.

This is my story. I hope it helps you. I couldn't tell all; the omissions protect the innocent and the not so innocent. That's another book entirely. Maybe that's the *next* one...

1

In My End Is My Beginning

The sound of a kiss rang out in the still room.

The dark was impenetrable, like thick, black velvet you could almost touch. I woke with a start, suddenly clearheaded as though I'd never been asleep.

Something was in the room—some living presence besides myself. I could feel it as plainly as I could feel my own heart thumping in my chest. The covers felt heavy, almost wet. They were wrapped around my legs, but I didn't want to move and let whatever it was know I was awake and aware.

The half-remembered psalm from my childhood came back to me, from a long-ago Sunday school in another life. *"Thou shalt not be afraid for the terror by night…"*

I moved my eyes toward the foot of the bed, to the space beyond it where the faint glow from the hall light leaked through the doorframe. My own breathing was the only noise I could hear now; I tried to keep it even and measured. That sense of pressure, as if someone was sitting on my chest, increased. It was a feeling I knew well from a lifetime of dealing with it.

The air in the room felt thick, another all-too familiar feeling. My skin tingled, almost as if a static charge surrounded me. I waited, remembering what had brought me from that place between semi-sleep and wakefulness to full attention.

There'd been a noise. A noise so familiar, so longed for, that I thought maybe I'd dreamt it. The sound of an air kiss, that silly smooching noise we always made to each other, a sentimental holdover from his childhood. All three of us had done it—his dad, James, and me. It was our call-and-response ever since James was old enough to understand the game. Whoever did it first was supposed to do it twice. That was usually me. James, sometimes half annoyed—especially after he'd grown up and left childish things behind—would usually bend the rules and only answer with one. Sometimes I had to do it a couple of times before he'd return it. But he knew it was important to me, a nostalgic reminder of his childhood, so most of the time he played along.

Alone in the dark, I waited expectantly, tingling all over, trying to calmly draw in breath through the dense atmosphere. Since I'd already heard it once, I decided I'd make the requisite double response. So I pursed my lips and kissed into the darkness twice.

With all my senses on high alert, I waited. Deep into that chilly autumn night, all alone in the dark of my room, the sound of my precious son returning my kiss rang out one time.

James, my beautiful, twenty-four-year-old, dark-haired, hazel-eyed son, had been dead fifteen months.

———

I'm a psychic, but mostly a reluctant one. My life's been filled with clairvoyance, dreams that came true, readings, ghosts, palmistry, and tarot. I was born psychic and I know I'd probably enjoy life more without the ability. But I wasn't given the choice.

I'm not the granola-eating hippie type you might associate with this. I'm not the New Age buzz-word-of-the-moment type either. I'm not interested in telling you about which crystals do what or how to find your past lives, wherever you may have left them. I don't always believe in the standard psychic fodder and often don't fit in with those who do. Sometimes I don't know what to make of them. I've realized other psychics don't know what to make of me either. With a fairly strong faith in God, I consider myself pretty traditional and almost conservative. I'm even a card-carrying member of the Daughters of the American Revolution. But I'm too Christian for the psychic world and too psychic for the Christian world. I'm stranded out here somewhere in-between.

My biggest fear over James's death has been that because of my lifelong experience with the paranormal—from the early days of questioning my abilities and searching for answers to finally accepting and even pursuing the psychic life—I may inadvertently have let something evil in, or at the very least, made myself a target. Maybe it was when I'd unwittingly asked for an Ouija board for Christmas when I was thirteen. Now there's an oxymoron: celebrate the birth of Christ with a gift that can let demonic forces in.

Maybe it happened at one of the paranormal investigations I've assisted with or at a house that I tried to clear of a presence. Maybe that was when something came in through the door between this world and the next. I truly hope not. I agonize over it. But the truth is I'll never know until I get to that next world.

I like to think I'm an average person. But my life has overflowed with two things that others usually don't have to this degree—musical and psychic abilities. I've been a professional musician since the age of sixteen, and I've always had psychic gifts.

When very young, I mostly had clairvoyance and prophetic dreams, such as the time I dreamed about a doll that had hair that "grew."

"I want that pretty doll with yellow hair," I told my mom at breakfast. "Her hair is short, and then you can make it grow really, really long."

"I thought you wanted Santa to bring you a Barbie with lots of outfits," Mom answered.

"No, I want the doll with the hair," I pouted, as only a six-year-old can. "She's beautiful."

I'd seen her in great detail and described her to Mom. When Christmas morning came, I rushed to open my presents from Santa, to find a red-haired, ponytailed Barbie instead. Mom must've seen my look of disappointment.

"Santa couldn't find your doll anywhere," she explained. "We asked him when we saw him at the department store."

When I was older, she told me they'd looked for it everywhere, assuming I'd seen it on TV in the weeks before Christmas. It wasn't until the following Christmas that *Tressy* came on the market. When I finally got her, it was exciting. I'd waited a long time.

As I got older, I always knew what people were going to say. I could barely listen to conversations, and when people talked to me, I only pretended to pay attention.

When I explained my annoyance to Mom, she told me to be polite, keep quiet, and not to appear to be a know-it-all. I'm not sure she understood that what I was experiencing was a psychic ability.

Not too surprisingly, when James was young, he came to me saying almost the exact same thing. I told him he might not know *exactly* what they were going to say.

"I do know, Mom," he replied, exasperated. "Stop trying to tell me I don't!"

So, after coaching him a little bit about using tact, as Mom had coached me, I let it drop.

Clairvoyance and claircognizance are the names of the feelings I get, of knowing something, such as impending danger, or someone's name. Clairaudience is when I hear something spoken in my head. Clairsentience means feeling things, like where a disease is located or the emotions of another person or place, and psychokinesis is affecting objects with the mind. At different times in my life, I've used each, though I didn't always understand I was using them. In my early teens, spirits came into my life—maybe the haunted house I moved into was caused by my careless use of an Ouija board. Or not. Either way, I became more curious about such things and began to study palmistry and tarot extensively as well.

I've been searching for the answers to faith and the metaphysical for a long time. I remember praying to Jesus as a little girl, wanting Him to write something, anything, on a little slip of paper that I'd tuck under my music box every night. Every morning I'd check it faithfully, certain that something would be there, since I totally believed He could do it. I finally gave up on getting direct evidence or answers, at least in this form. So I kept searching for other ways.

On an intellectual level, I've spent years trying to understand all this. I have a few theories for my conclusions, but I'm still learning, and still searching. James is still teaching me.

————

What's it like being a real psychic? Some nights, when I lie in bed in the dark, trying to fall asleep, I hear voices that I can't quite understand. The continual rising and falling cadence of conversation is just under the audible range of hearing. I run a window fan to block the sounds because I don't *want* to hear it. Thankfully, it doesn't happen constantly or it'd drive me crazy. I believe sometimes I'm picking up the stray thoughts of others, and at times, I think they're the voices of those who've passed on—from the spirit world.

When I walk into a room full of people, I can sometimes feel who's angry, and when talking to someone, I can usually feel the unspoken agenda. Sometimes I can feel lies, tension, anger, or fear, coming from various points in a crowded room. But I never know if the guy sitting in the corner is a serial killer ready to strike or just someone who had a fight with his wife. It's exhausting at times, because it keeps me hypervigilant, unable to relax. When I was young, I tried to shut all this off by anesthetizing myself with various substances, but that only put off what I eventually had to face.

Over time I've learned that the feelings can't *be* completely turned off. To keep my sanity, I've learned how to withdraw the psychic antennae to mute the noise. The problem is, it all feels like a warning, even when there's nothing to warn about. It's just as much a burden as a gift. I also understand when people are skeptical. Even after all this time, I sometimes can hardly believe it myself. I'm always looking for the scientific causes behind the phenomena and for proof of other supposed psychics' abilities. I know it's real, because I have it; I guess I'm searching for what is "normal" for other psychics. But I haven't found many other real psychics. They're as rare as hen's teeth, as Grandma used to say.

———

I've thought a lot about when I first knew I was different. When it's always been with you, there *is* no defining moment. It's hard to pinpoint when I first realized others don't feel this way or have these things happen. One thing I *have* noticed is that psychic abilities run in families. I know they do in mine.

I was born into a loving family. My dad got into the sixties plastics craze early, becoming superintendent of a factory. He was a hard worker, intelligent, easygoing, and fun. Mom was the traditional 1950s stay-at-home housewife who ruled the roost with an iron fist in a velvet glove. Yet she was also very childlike.

My folks grew up in the same rural area. As teens, they lived down the road from each other, and after a somewhat obstructed courtship due to the watchful eye of my religious grandma, they got married in the late 1940s. They had my sister Brooke, and I was the middle child, followed by my little brother Dane.

My dad's ancestors came from Ireland in 1830. From a musical family, he played guitar and piano, which explains my musical abilities. At sixteen, my Dad was playing music for money, just as I was, and James too.

Mom came from a larger family, which survived by farming. With eight kids to feed, they lived through lean times. My psychic abilities can be traced to her side. Her mom's mother was a Nutter, descendant of Alice Nutter, one of the infamous Lancashire witches executed by King James in August 1612. I've always wondered if poor Lady Alice had the psychic streak, too. They didn't take kindly to that in those days, or anything that smacked of witchcraft. She was chained to the floor in Lancaster Castle while awaiting her turn at the gallows. Mom's paternal grandmother was a full-blooded Cherokee Indian, a race traditionally believed to have closer ties to the intuitive side of this world. Mom's bloodline was evident in her straight, black hair and high cheekbones.

Probably the oddest thing about mom's family being psychic was the fact that they were also very religious, and she raised us the same way. Strict Protestants descended from Quakers, we attended church faithfully while growing up, and I can still quote scripture with the best of 'em!

Mom's family considered psychic abilities one of God's gifts, like prophecy of biblical times. They accepted it and never questioned it, apparently knowing they were right with God. Then again, none of them hung out their psychic shingle either. They downplayed the abilities and didn't talk openly about them, but it was an accepted family fact. To me, it felt as though they considered it shameful. Maybe they did, in light of what happened to Alice Nutter.

Just before any family member passed away, Mom and Grandma had dreams of a large white bird. Grandma would quietly announce "The Dream," usually at her kitchen table, which served as a gathering place for the extended family.

Having lots of aunts, uncles, and cousins was one of the perks of Gram's having eight children. She was a tiny woman, wise and yet superstitious. We all loved and respected her—she didn't have to raise her voice to be heard. As soon as she spoke, all noise and bustle would cease. Kids would go silent, eyes would grow large, and everyone would wait to hear about "The Dream." One of the adults would respectfully clear their throat and ask a question.

"Did it come in through the window?" my uncle would ask.

"Yes," Grandma answered, "just like always."

"Was it white?" he'd continue.

"Yes," she'd reply.

He'd nod quietly, head down.

We all knew what this meant and all eyes would glance about the room, from child to adult, from young to old. Who would it be? This ritual had been going on for a very long time—since Gram's grandmother, maybe before. It was proven. It was accurate. It was *scary*.

Usually within three or four days, we got word of a death. Most often it was an older relative we didn't know, which was easier to cope with.

There were always signs and omens: Too many crows in a nearby tree? Not good. A bird got in the house? Even worse. Everything was significant, though not always explained. You'd just get "the look" from Grandma, and the fear began.

Thanks to Grandma, my family also knew when to go on trips and when to play it safe and stay home. Pity anyone who dared scoff at her advice. The one time my dad didn't heed Gram's warning, we were in a wreck. After that chilling incident, Dad became a lifelong believer.

It was all too mysterious and unfathomable, and when it *was* spoken of, it was in the hushed, reverent tones reserved for churches and funeral homes.

———

I've worked as a psychic for many years. I spend a lot of time helping with relationship difficulties, but I've also done everything from helping find lost pets to diagnosing unknown health conditions. I've clairvoyantly been shown everything from diseased kidneys and early stage cancers to heart blockages, gallstones, and polyps. And though I've never taken anatomy classes, I've always been able to figure out what I'm being shown. I simply close my eyes and "the light" forms pictures for me.

I like to focus on the *good* these psychic abilities have done over the years. Sometimes friends have been helped. Recently while on the phone with one who was on the interstate, I suddenly got a bad feeling.

"Where are you?" I asked him, trying to make sense of the feeling of danger.

"I'm just above the weigh station, why?"

"I'm getting a very bad feeling," I told him. "Please be careful."

"Okay, I'm slowing down," he said, lifting his foot off the accelerator, then he shouted, "Oh my God!"

"What, what?" I yelled.

"As I let up on the gas, I dropped behind the car in front of me, and the one beside me in the passing lane. A deer just bolted into the road and the guy passing me hit it and spun into my lane! If I hadn't slowed down, he would've hit me!"

My friend watched in the rearview mirror as the driver stopped and got out, proving he was okay. But it might not have turned out so well had he been beside my friend's car.

"Thank you," he said. "You may have just saved my life, or at the very least, spared me a serious wreck."

My friend had always believed in my gifts, especially after dreams that came to pass and things predicted that happened. After the incident on the freeway, he realized how important it was to listen to every bad feeling, no matter how strange.

———

As a psychic, I'm often called to work on paranormal investigations, or to confirm or deny the presence of a spirit in a house. I've investigated small apartments and large public buildings, factories and graveyards, sometimes trying to clear any presence found—that is, if they *want* to be cleared. In the end, it's really up to them. Just like the people they used to be, they make up their own minds.

I volunteer at historical sites, doing readings for special events, and I do free readings on metaphysical websites. I was given these abilities for some reason, and I believe it's to help others.

I've been recruited by the psychic lines—the largest, the oldest, and most highly rated—but I just don't have time to meet their minimum hour requirements.

I work occasionally as a reader for Haunted Heartland Tours, which specializes in ghost hunts at haunted locations, owned by friend, author, and paranormal investigator Sherri Brake. I also have a large private clientele.

Many say that psychic abilities and creativity are inter-twined, with the most common theory being that right-brained creative people are more open and childlike, hence more receptive. This is why artistic types seem to have abilities at a higher rate than the rest of the population, and also why children often have them. They often see spirits when adults can't, but usually grow out of it.

————

I've always believed that everyone has some degree of psychic ability, and that often a childhood trauma will hone and develop it out of necessity—almost as another sense—to keep us safe. I didn't realize until I was older and had done research, that this belief is held by many in the paranormal field. In my own case, I was six, and in the first grade, when my safe, peaceful little world was shattered.

"Scoot your desks together in groups of three," directed our teacher one day.

There was a boy in our class who'd had a severe head trauma and hadn't been quite right since. He didn't bathe often enough, smelled bad, and was always causing trouble.

This boy was in my group of three desks. I clearly remember standing shyly by as the teacher helped everyone. I remember the girl beside me saying, "I don't want to sit with him, HE STINKS!"

The boy had his back to us, and apparently he thought I said it. He whirled around and in a flash, ripped the semi-stiff plastic headband from my hair, and somehow wrapped it around my throat, pulling on both ends, strangling me, until the headband broke. Later, I realized he must've used considerable force to break it this way. The teacher didn't see what was going on and couldn't do anything to prevent it. I was so traumatized that I don't remember anything that followed—except that the teacher felt bad enough to buy me a bag full of headbands later.

I also don't remember my mom making a fuss about it, and wonder if she even knew. When I remembered the incident as an adult, she had no memory of it.

Later in life, I began having recurring nightmares; it had such a traumatic effect, I'd repressed it most of my life. This one incident taught me I wasn't safe and that any moment, I could be violently attacked and killed, and no one could save me. Not parents, not teachers; no one. I was on my own.

This crucial event turned a shy, sensitive child even further inward. So began the process of needing to rely on an already inherited "sixth sense," which was reinforced over the next few years by my parents moving often, sending me into what felt like dangerous new places. From second through fifth grade, we moved every year. One year we moved twice. Always the new kid on the block, always getting used to new schools, and always living in fear of another attacker. No wonder I was nervous.

2

Surviving
Hell House

When we were very little, like most kids, we opened our presents Christmas morning. And like most kids, we believed Santa brought them. At some point, our more knowledgeable classmates told us that Santa was a myth, and that it was our parents who bought the presents.

Being older when I first heard this, I wasn't upset. But I didn't want my eight-year-old brother Dane to know. I did all I could to keep his belief alive. I wrote tiny, elflike notes and positioned them on an ornament on our tree. The notes were written by "Jo-Jo the Elf" and they fueled Dane's excitement.

Finally, in the third grade, Dane learned that Santa wasn't real. Once the truth was out, I begged our parents for an early present the following Christmas Eve. Dane pushed for it too. Together we won, and opening one present on Christmas Eve turned into a yearly tradition.

That first Christmas Eve, I grabbed a box that contained an Ouija board. The Ouija board had been advertised heavily. I thought it sounded pretty neat, and its promise that we'd be able to "mystify our friends" hooked me instantly.

"Look, a Ouija!" I yelled at Dane. (We pronounced it Weejee.)

My brother, brow furrowed and deeply engrossed in a new truck, couldn't be bothered. "Cool," he mumbled, hoping I'd go away.

With auburn hair and a smattering of freckles across his nose, Dane was my beloved little brother. He was a smaller version of me, and we were both miniature versions of Dad. Dane was smart, at least two years beyond his chronological age. As with most younger siblings, sometimes he bugged me, but most of the time I was fiercely protective.

"C'mon, let's try it out," I insisted, but all Dane wanted to do was play with his truck. After a half hour of relentless pleading, he finally gave in.

"Okay, it says you put your fingers on this thingy, like this," I said, as I showed him how to lay fingers on the planchette. "Then, you're supposed to ask a question," I continued enthusiastically.

"Like what?" Dane asked.

I thought long and hard as we sat face to face, considering each other, fingers on the board between us. "Okay, how about this? Is anyone out there? If you can hear me, can you please come here and talk to me? Can you come be my friend?"

Eyes locked on the board, we waited expectantly for the planchette to move. One minute passed, then two. Nothing was happening. Doing his best to hide his boredom, Dane patiently waited for me to make the next move.

I asked again, "If you can hear me, can you please come talk?" We both stared at the board and waited. Suddenly there was a crash from the kitchen. We jumped up and ran to the kitchen to find a pan had fallen out of the cupboard, where it was securely stored. Dane looked from the pan to me and back, puzzled. I knew what he was thinking: "Did we do that?" I laughed nervously, not knowing what to say—or what to believe.

Thankfully, Mom and Dad returned home only minutes afterward. I quickly put the Ouija back in its box and tossed it in a closet where it was forgotten. How could a pan falling out of a cupboard be due to the Ouija board? The thing didn't even work. We never mentioned the incident again.

———

My mom was the restless type—and the reason we moved every two or three years. She was happiest when engrossed in decorating a new home. Dad adored her and went along with anything she wanted. He himself was a bit of a gypsy, excited by a change of scene. Only weeks after the Ouija incident, Mom found a house that she wanted on Fifth Street. The Ouija moved with us. I remember seeing it in the back of my closet, though we never used it again. But just as you can't put toothpaste back in the tube, some doors, once opened, remain open.

I was fourteen, my sister Brooke was eighteen, and Dane was ten when we moved to Fifth Street. With three bedrooms upstairs, and a family room, parlor, and bathroom downstairs off the kitchen, it was similar to other homes in the area.

A couple of weeks after moving in, I discovered that our new home only *looked* like all the other houses on the street.

A scrawny tomboy often mistaken for a boy, I'd finally let my auburn hair grow long so I'd look more feminine. I was desperate to fit in, have friends, and later on, maybe even a boyfriend. Recently, boys had come onto my radar, though I was too shy to do anything about it. They were still too scary.

It didn't take us long to make friends in our new neighborhood. We were allowed to have sleepovers on Friday nights, so my brother and I took turns. We'd usually stay up half the night watching cheesy 1950s sci-fi films.

Kim, my new best friend, was my first sleepover. We spread blankets and pillows on the living room floor to watch the movie, eat potato chips, but mostly talk about boys. That first sleepover, Brooke and Dane were staying at friends' houses and my parents were asleep upstairs. Kim and I had the downstairs to ourselves. While the black-and-white movie flickered on the TV, we chatted.

"So, do you think Corey likes me?" Kim asked, twisting a strand of her long blonde hair around her finger.

"I heard he was talking to Stacy outside study hall," I told her, "but you're so much cuter than her." I studied Kim as she fluffed her hair. I envied her. She was a girly-girl, but pretty cool even so, and I wanted to be just like her. She was pretty and popular.

I heard a soft knocking begin during lulls in conversation. Just a few knocks, at the top of the wall near the ceiling. Then they suddenly jumped to the opposite wall, and I felt the hair on my arms stand up as the room got colder. Kim had to have heard the noises, but they didn't seem to upset her enough to stop talking. *What could be causing this? No way am I mentioning it, especially if Kim hasn't noticed.*

"Troy seems to make excuses to be around *you* an awful lot," she continued.

The knocks grew louder and more insistent; like knuckles on plaster, muffled at first, then sharper, quicker, leaping around the room, jumping from ceiling to walls at random. It was obvious no human being could be doing this. It was too fast, too unpredictable. For several moments, I felt shackled to the floor. I couldn't think, the fear overwhelming me. The room was freezing, and all the hair on my body was on end, as though I was bathed in static electricity. Kim stopped talking and looked at the ceiling and around at the corners of the room.

"Hey, what's making that noise?" she asked. "Brrr, it's cold in here all of a sudden!"

"I don't know," I replied, darting nervous glances from her to the ceiling. "Maybe it's the dog upstairs." I'd dealt with psychic feelings before, but this was something else entirely!

Something was in the room with us! I felt watched and laughed at. The air was heavy, and I couldn't get my breath. My left side began to tingle, almost like a cold chill was running up and down it, and I started to feel sick to my stomach. Drowning in a kind of indescribable fear and dread, I tried to remain calm as my mind struggled to make sense of what was happening. I didn't want Kim to tell the whole school I was a weirdo who lived in a haunted house. But it was too late. With eyes wide, we huddled together on the living room floor, her expression frozen into an inscrutable mask.

Gradually, the knocks grew fainter and finally stopped. For twenty tense minutes we'd been surrounded by what I can only call evil, but finally it began to dissipate. As though it had run out of steam.

"Wow," Kim whispered, "that was really weird."

Oh great, I thought.

As expected, friends soon knew about the weird noises—and that no way did they come from the dog upstairs.

Despite this, I still begged friends to come in with me after school. My mom had taken a part-time job and I didn't want to go into the house alone.

"Why don't you come in for a minute while I change?" I asked Kim, as we approached Fifth Street. "My mom just made cookies, you can have some while you wait... it'll only take me a minute."

"No way," she replied. "But I'll wait outside if you bring some out."

With no backup, I raced into my house, grabbed a handful of cookies, ran back out to give them to her, then bolted back in. I ran upstairs to my room, flung off my clothes, eyes squeezed shut, and pulled on my everyday clothes, all the while singing at the top of my lungs as if I didn't have a care in the world. I thought that music might magically render me invisible—and invisible equaled invincible. "They" might not notice me if I didn't act scared. I also felt braver knowing Kim could hear me singing from the porch. Once in my play clothes, I ran back downstairs and out, slamming the door behind me.

I desperately wanted to pretend this stuff wasn't happening, but despite all attempts to appear normal and play down what was going on at my house, the knocking continued. By now, others experienced it. The knocking happened many times on sleepovers with friends. It became a struggle between wanting to keep my shameful haunted house a secret, and wanting another human being there with me to give me courage. And sometimes the knocking was the precursor to more frightening phenomena.

———

My little brother Dane was the budding mad scientist of the family. Smart and constantly curious, he set up a laboratory in the basement, which could only be accessed by raising a hatch-type door on the back porch, then descending steep, narrow stairs into the dank rooms below. At home with cables snaking across the hard-packed dirt floor, Dane spent countless hours down there—both alone and with friends—often working deep into the night designing and assembling everything from stink bombs to model rockets. Sometimes when he descended into his lab, it would be thick with the presence of some dark energy. Other times, it felt normal. However, due to the creepiness I felt, I never went down to the lab.

There were several smaller rooms off the lab. Mom kept cans of food on some old shelves in one small room. A group of old mason jars left by some previous occupant were also there, covered in dust.

Sometimes while Dane was working in his lab, he'd hear cans being picked up and put down. He'd hear them being slid across the rough, wooden shelves, a sound that defied explanation.

"Mom?" he'd yell out. Sometimes she'd hear him yell from way above in the house, and she'd yell back. Many times he'd get up quietly and check to see if she'd come down to get a can of something for supper. But no one was ever there, only that thick, dark energy enveloping the tiny room. That heavy atmosphere was always a good indicator of whether Dane would hear the cans moving on any particular day.

Sometimes Dane heard a huge crash—the sound of breaking glass, *lots* of glass. The first time it happened, thinking the old, dusty jars and the shelves had fallen, he ran to look. No sign of anything, not even a shard of glass. After a few times, he finally stopped checking. Many of his friend's sleepovers ended with them leaving in the middle of the night. Whether from homesickness or fear, he never knew.

One evening, after Mom painted the back porch slab a battleship gray and roped off the area with wet paint signs, there were footprints in the still-tacky paint the next morning. The prints appeared to be from old worn shoes, and they came from the basement hatch. They walked over to the window, like they were looking in. But there were no footprints going back the way they came. They just ended at the window. The thought that "someone" I couldn't see was still standing there scared me to death. The next thought, that this "someone" either flew away or disappeared, was even worse.

And the knocking continued.

Around this same time, everyone in the house began seeing a woman walk by the doorway to the parlor. She was only visible from the corners of our eyes, and when we turned, she was gone. She was very dark, seemingly dressed in a long black skirt and blouse, gliding along just out of range, always one step ahead of us. Almost everyone who came in the house saw her at some point. But she was harmless compared to other things. Dane and I eventually compared notes, and started to complain that we wanted to move. But our parents hadn't yet seen or felt what we did. We discussed things away from the house mostly; I was afraid to speak of them inside it. I'd go silent with fear if anyone mentioned ghosts. I thought I could feel them watching me.

I'll never forget the first time Dad heard what we called "squeaky wheels." Until that day, he'd had a hard time believing our stories because he didn't experience them. That was understandable because he worked all day, and was in bed not long after dinner, asleep as soon as his head hit the pillow.

It was a beautiful fall day, and a slight breeze swirled the leaves around us while we raked in our small front yard. The upstairs window in my bedroom was open, as was my brother's window in the adjacent room. Dad and I were alone; everyone else had gone to the store.

As soon as the noise began, he stopped raking. It sounded like a large, heavy Victorian dresser with squeaky wooden wheels being rolled across the floor, from my room into my brother's. The sound was so clear I could almost feel the weight of it as it lumbered and squeaked across the length of the upstairs rooms. Dad had tried so hard to convince us the noises were probably coming from the neighbor's, but I'll never forget the look on his face that day. This event changed him.

"There it is, there it is. Do you hear it?" I yelled.

"I believe you now," he said, staring at me in shock.

As the frequency and intensity of events at Fifth Street increased, I became obsessed with finding out about the paranormal. I searched libraries and bookstores, amassing a collection with my allowance, reading everything I could about subjects from near-death experiences to poltergeists.

I learned about residual hauntings, which don't interact with you, but play the same scenes over and over, like a tape loop. Intelligent hauntings were ghosts who could interact and try to get your attention. Poltergeists, "noisy ghosts," moved things, threw things, and scared the bejesus out of you—and the jury was still out if they could be caused by someone entering puberty. And finally there were demonic infestations, which seemed like a combination of all three but had evil intentions because of their hatred of all God's creations. I became the expert on occult matters among my friends. I became a nervous wreck as well.

One night, my sister Brooke and I were sitting on the sofa. Everyone else was sleeping. I was reading and Brooke was brushing out a hairpiece when the knocking started. We glanced at each other, too terrified to say anything that might draw "its" attention. And we pretended to go back to our tasks, though on high alert.

But apparently it wanted our attention—a soft, jumbled cacophony of moans and voices began building, surrounding us in different pitches and cadences. The sounds came from everywhere and nowhere, engulfing us. Mumbling, chuckling, and groaning, they grew louder and louder, building to a crescendo like something from the depths of hell. It was a human sound made horrifyingly inhuman because it came from a hundred voices in a room where we were utterly alone.

Bolting up, Brooke and I pushed and struggled to be the first up the stairs to my parents' room. Once Dad established that there was no burglar, and once again our haunted house was the culprit, we all tried to go back to sleep. I slept on the floor in my parents' room, a place that became my refuge.

When a bout of stomach flu was making the rounds, feeling slightly ill, I decided to sleep downstairs near the bathroom, just in case. I was on the sofa with my eyes closed, feeling sicker by the minute. "*I'm not going to throw up*," I told myself over and over, hoping to make it so, when suddenly there was the sound of shuffling feet on carpet. They began walking around the coffee table, right beside me! Once again, the room went ice cold and I felt my hair stand up. At first I thought my brother or sister had come to check on me, but one glance told me there was no one else in the room. A bolt of fear shot through me; *it was in the room with me!* Round and round went the footsteps, as I squeezed my eyes shut, frozen in terror. After the fourth or fifth time around, I ran screaming for the stairs—back to the refuge of Mom and Dad's room.

Hard as I wished for peace and normalcy, the terrifying events continued. One night after Brooke got married and moved out, I went through my usual pre-bedtime routine. I now had the bedroom we'd shared to myself, which was great in some ways. But I soon realized there was a price for such privacy: I was alone. But not really.

Tucked into bed, I quietly thought about school the next day: what to wear, what my friends and I'd planned— when suddenly I was interrupted by an odd sensation and even odder sound. *Scritch, scritch, scritch.* Down near my right foot, under the covers, something was scratching on the fitted sheet on my mattress, sending the vibration up through my body. It was the sound of invisible fingernails, and they were under my covers with me! Once again, I ran screaming to my parents' room.

It had been scary enough in the living room, but being attacked in the intimacy of my bedroom drove me to the edge. It was psychological terror at its worst, wearing me down little by little. Not long after the scratching incident, while lying in bed, I felt someone drum their fingers on my forehead, from pinky to index finger, just as you would on a table. The atmosphere was so thick it was palpable. It was the ultimate in horror to wonder if something thought this was funny, scaring me so badly. Unable to breathe, in panic, I rushed to Mom and Dad's room, where I stayed for several more nights.

Despite the fact that I was quietly becoming a nervous wreck, I was determined to keep my daily terror hidden, an unmentionable secret from most of my acquaintances, except for my new boyfriend. I'd met him when he was an usher at my sister's wedding. I loved finally having a boyfriend. *Having a boyfriend makes me normal*, I thought. *If nothing else, I want to appear normal!*

One night, we were sitting on the couch in the family room watching TV. He dozed off, sitting upright, so I did my best to be quiet as I got up to use the bathroom—in the next room, in the corner of the kitchen. Instead of a lock, the bathroom door had a hook and eye latch. If the door wasn't latched, it swung open on its own. When I was done, I unhooked the latch and gave the door a gentle push as usual, but it stuck fast. Confused, I leaned into it hard, but it wouldn't budge.

My boyfriend's playing a joke on me, I thought; *he's holding it on the other side.* Laughing, I pushed it as hard as I could to try and show him I was no wimpy girl. Again, it didn't budge.

"All right, very funny, let me out now," I said through the door. No answer. Well, I wouldn't act like an idiot and push it again. I was done playing games. For a good thirty seconds, I stood anxiously twisting his class ring, before I disgustedly gave the door a little brush with my hand, and it swung open. "Great," I said, expecting to see him standing there with a big smirk on his face.

No one was there.

I hurried back to the front room, and there he was sleeping in the same position I'd left him. This had to be a joke; he'd somehow silently run back and was now pretending to sleep.

"Very funny," I said loudly, pushing his shoulder. Up jerked his head; I'd awakened him from a deep sleep. No way could he fake it that well.

This haunting had become personal. It was focused on terrifying me. This was almost too much to bear, living in absolute terror wondering what it would decide to do next. I felt alone with it.

I was soon relieved to get away from the house on a trip out West with my family to visit my sister in Las Vegas. It was a magical trip, made more so by leaving behind the horror. I also found a little dog I named Cryer, a three-month-old stray hanging around my sister's place.

I stayed the weekend with Brooke while Mom and Dad went to visit relatives in California. By the time they came back to pick me up, I'd fallen in love with little Cryer. I lied and told Mom she was housebroken, and we were inseparable after that; Cryer was my closest friend and constant companion. I felt I could face the haunting when hugging her close to me. I carried her around in a little cloth purse, long before Paris was a Hilton! And when we got home, the house resumed right where it left off. And Cryer stared and barked at something in my room each night about three a.m.

At first, my folks had pooh-poohed the whole haunted thing. "There's no such thing as ghosts," Mom protested. "I don't know what has gotten into you kids."

It made no sense to her that we were having these problems—nothing like this had ever happened to us before; and this was the seventh house we'd moved into, at least since I'd been old enough to remember. Although Mom was psychic herself, she was convinced we were imagining it all. Her strict religious background had taught her demons caused these things, but I don't think she was ready to accept that possibility! She was soon to meet whatever it was firsthand—when she was awakened at night by an old man bending over her, staring into her face. After it happened several times, and after hearing the same crashing sounds my brother heard while she was alone in the house, she too was afraid and began to waver in her beliefs. Once Dad also heard the squeaky wheels, they weren't so quick to dismiss our experiences.

But to appear normal, Mom still publicly toed the party line. One summer evening, my sister's in-laws visited. They were a likeable couple, had values very similar to ours, and my parents liked them.

We were all sitting in the parlor, which continued to feel like the most haunted room in the house, when my brother brought up the ghosts. "It's all in their imagination," quipped Mom, embarrassed, quickly seconded by Brooke's new father-in-law, declaring, "There's no such thing as ghosts."

"Be careful, we have to live here with it," I said uneasily. I was so terrified, I could barely allow myself to *think* about the ghosts, let alone acknowledge them out loud!

Fed up with this foolishness, Brooke's father-in-law stared at me and loudly declared, "If there's anyone or anything in this house other than the people in this room, give me a sign. I dare you, because I don't believe in you!"

An ominous hush seemed to fall over the house. *Uh oh*, I thought. And as we all got very quiet, I braced myself. I knew what it was capable of.

But Brooke's father-in-law sat there in the heavy up-holstered swivel rocker in the corner, grinning! After about thirty seconds, he burst out, "See, I told you so!" And just as he uttered the word "so," the heavy rocker tipped over backwards, dumping him unceremoniously in the corner!

Could he have done this on purpose—his idea of a joke? I thought. One look at his panic-stricken face and I knew that wasn't the case. The chair weighed over one hundred pounds, and all the times we'd sat in it, swiveled in it, and even had younger relatives jumping in it, it had never tipped over. Our new relative by marriage was completely dismayed. Gone was his usual genial composure. Unglued, he sat white-faced for a few minutes, answering Mom and Dad's solicitous questions.

"Are you sure you're okay? Did you hit your head on the wall?"

"I'm fine," he replied. "I must have overbalanced when I leaned back."

But he *hadn't* leaned back. Lamely he tried to make up reasons why it happened, until finally he gave some excuse to leave early, and made a hasty exit. In the three years we lived there, he never came back.

———

Not long afterwards, Mom and Dad decided to move out of Fifth Street as well. I remember my dread the first time I walked into their new house. With my chest constricted, posture hunched, and totally shell-shocked from the haunting, I feared the new house might be the same. Slowly I opened myself; cautiously I walked through the house, even up into the attic, just to be sure. Nothing. Just a couple of wasps humming lazily in the summer warmth. That peaceful, benevolent feeling was such an incredible relief after the malevolence of Fifth Street. It still took me quite a while to believe I was safe there. Fifth Street scarred me badly.

Over the years, I never stopped thinking about the house on Fifth Street. I've often wanted to return with the knowledge I now have. A few years ago, I learned that my son James had a friend who'd lived there for a while. We ran into him one day, and I tactfully tried to ask about his experiences without alarming him.

"No, I never had anything happen to me there," he said indifferently, "but my little sister was very scared and told us things were happening to her. We didn't believe her."

Maybe the presence there only focuses on young girls. Or maybe his sister has a little bit of "the gift," which some believe can attract spirits and energies. It's said they see those with abilities "like a light in a dark room." Either way, Fifth Street changed my life. I began seriously study-ing the occult, needing to understand what had happened to me. At the same time, I continued my budding music career, which funded my research into this hidden world.

And once I started, I couldn't help but keep inves-tigating. After I completed the first draft of this book, something so strange happened that I just had to call my editor to "stop the presses" and include it. After over seven decades, the 1940 census was released to the public. I got on the website this morning to find the occupants of Fifth Street seventy-two years ago. Shock washed over me at what I read—the surname of my great-grandmother's family! Her brother's son, my Grandpa's first cousin, was living there with his wife and son in 1940! The son was thirteen at the time and is now eighty-five—and he still lives here in town. I had to call him.

"Hello Mr. Deems," I greeted him, explaining my mission carefully.

"My dad was your second cousin," I told him, "and we lived in your old house on Fifth Street many years after you. I really had a rough time there because I thought the house was haunted."

Luckily, he didn't hang up, and didn't seem to think I was crazy.

"I absolutely hated that upstairs," he told me. "There were no lights upstairs at that time, and I had to walk through my parent's room to get to mine." As he described his bedroom, I realized it was the bedroom I'd had. He said he heard noises, and was scared of the upstairs, but back in those days he had to be careful, because they'd tease a boy unmercifully for being a scaredy-cat. Then he told me something that really made me wonder. His mother's sister died in the parlor, and her maiden name was another family surname. From my research, I believe this was another cousin. Maybe because I was a relative, and psychic, this woman's spirit tried to get my attention. Maybe she was the lady we always saw. Or maybe it was my great-grandma, attracted to her descendants in the house. I imagined the spirit/s wandering lost all those years until we moved in, and suddenly recognizing us or realizing that they could "see" me. I was too young and scared to understand they may have wanted to communicate.

We said our goodbyes and I thanked him. I truly don't know what happened at Fifth Street. Maybe it was a mixture of several things. The haunting was poltergeist-like in nature, which many believe are caused by a preteen, particularly a female. I don't know if I believe that theory because it seemed so personal. My new findings do give me another possible scenario, though. It only took four decades to add this twist to the story of Fifth Street.

This early experience still affects me, and I have a healthy respect for spirits to this day. They can still scare me, though not to the degree the Fifth Street spirits did. If I'd only asked to be left alone, that might have worked, but I was too young and too scared. I didn't even know I *could* ask.

———

That last year at Fifth Street felt like being caught in a downward spiral, a vortex determined to suck the normalcy out of my life. And all I wanted was to be normal—or at least like most other teens. I was searching for my place in the world, trying to figure out who I was and what I wanted, and maybe teenage craziness combined with the forces at Fifth Street created something bigger than what others my age had to contend with.

My first boyfriend provided a distraction and escape—not only from the haunted house, but from myself. I hated school, couldn't relate to any of it, and felt I didn't really need it. I listened to a lot of speeches about being an "underachiever," but I just didn't have the patience for anything that wasn't interesting. I'd been playing guitar for a couple years, which *was* interesting, and I began to play for money at various local events. It was a great part-time job.

Music allowed me to create something positive in my life, to focus on something other than the terrifying events at Fifth Street. In near-total absorption, I rehearsed for hours. It distracted me and kept my mind off the ghosts. Music became my obsession, my lifeline.

Feeling somewhat lost between my brother and sister—the cherished son and the favorite first daughter—and my parents' all-consuming love affair, I developed a desperate need to be heard. Though I didn't know this was driving me, I later realized music temporarily filled this need. For a little while, an audience "loved" me, and gave approval and affection. If I played well enough, I could make them happy. So I had to be the best I could be, I just had to be. Neurotic, I know, but it does seem a truism among most serious musicians.

At the age of seventeen, I told my parents I was quitting school to marry after my junior year. I decided I'd just not show up for my senior year—a subtle revenge of sorts. I felt grown-up. Mom married Dad at the same age— though those were very different times—maybe that's why they agreed. Or maybe it was just easier. My parents had a fifty-year love affair, and we kids were the natural by-products. They focused on each other, and though strict on some things, we had freedom in others.

The day of my wedding, pulling up to church and looking at my husband-to-be is a moment frozen in time. It was late summer, hot and humid, and my long gypsy dress was sticky against my skin. *I don't really wanna get married,* I thought. *I don't know if I love him enough to marry him, but I can't get out of it now or my parents will be disappointed.* And so I went through with it. And that's how I escaped Fifth Street.

After a year in California, our little family consisting of Cryer and my new husband, it became obvious he and I were best friends who got married and shouldn't have. I longed to restart back where I'd left off in my desperation to escape the haunted house. I wanted to play music and follow my dreams. We moved back to Ohio, but I couldn't be the one to break it off.

Luckily for us both, after another year, he decided it wasn't working and though I was sad, I knew he was right. We were too young and neither of us had the tools to make a relationship work. I moved back home with my parents, and it was as if those two years of marriage were a temporary glitch. But I was aware that marrying my first and only boyfriend at age seventeen to escape a haunted house wasn't something most girls need to do. I felt like a cog in the works of a much larger machine. I tried not to think about the guilt of broken vows. I was free.

A younger friend starting her senior year talked me into enrolling with her class, to finish school. I only needed a half day of classes for half the year to graduate. I instantly forgot about being a worldly married woman; I fit right in. There were several others in my class who were also nineteen, having been held back. And school was fun now; we went to parties, hung out, and chased boys!

Sometimes when I think back, I wonder if the forces at work at Fifth Street caused some of my rebellion. I was focusing more and more on the paranormal and things that exist just beyond our ability to see. It seemed as though everywhere I turned, I was confronted by more proof. Not that I really needed or wanted any more. Once you experience something of this nature, there's no going back. It changes everything. It's hard to believe until it happens to you, then it opens doors to amazing possibilities, and closes doors on previously held beliefs. Maybe we can all use a little bit of that, scary or not, but I wouldn't wish the haunted house method of enlightenment on my worst enemy!

3

Here a Ghost, There a Ghost

Toward the end of my life-changing experience at Fifth Street, my psychic grandma found an old abandoned mansion on the south side of town. After Grandpa passed away, she decided to sell their strawberry farm. Having raised eight kids, she was drawn to large houses, and this one was no exception.

I drove Mom and Grandma on that crisp late-fall afternoon when she got the keys to the new place. As we pulled up in front of the dark, brooding stone and brick Victorian home on Second Street, I felt a twinge of uneasiness. With a classic mansard roof and large wraparound porch with stone columns, it looked like the haunted houses in the movies. As I followed the sidewalk around to the back porch, I peered up at the towering stone mansion and thought I saw movement in one of the shaded narrow windows. Was something watching us? The wind kicked up a few leaves that blew past us, and I shuddered and wrapped my arms around myself at the sudden chill.

"Grandma, the windows in the basement are all broken out here," I announced, shocked. She was hard of hearing then, and later on, as deaf as a post, so I had to raise my voice a little. We could always tell on approach to Grandma's house if she was home by the sheer volume of whichever TV preacher she was watching that day.

"It's been abandoned for a long time, Debbie," she said. "There's gonna be a lot of work to do."

I squatted beside one of the broken basement windows to look inside as she and Mom fumbled with the padlock on the back door. Light from the windows on the opposite side of the house lit up the basement, filled with dirt and scattered bricks, and I gave a little shriek at what I saw.

"There's a dead cat down there," I yelled, "and dead birds!" The cat was shriveled and emaciated, one eye staring balefully up at me. "He probably went after the birds, then couldn't get back out," I said to no one in particular, as Mom and Grandma had already disappeared inside the house. *Dead cat,* I thought, *bad omen. Dead birds; even worse.*

I stepped into the kitchen at the back of the house and surveyed the debris on the floor, the old plaster walls, and the fifteen-foot ceilings. It smelled unpleasant, a cross between old, wet plaster caused by a leaky roof, and mildew. I hugged myself tighter as I hurried to follow the sounds of Mom and Grandma somewhere in the bowels of the house.

"Kathryn, this room would be just beautiful wallpapered," Grandma said to Mom.

"Yes, it really would," Mom answered. "I could start out there in the hallway and bring it all the way into this room." She pointed toward the front of the house, where the massive front door led to a foyer beside an open stairway. My mom was the interior decorator of the family, willing to hang wallpaper at the drop of a hat.

The wraparound porch had a door that opened into the room they were standing in. This would be Gram's TV and sitting room.

I have a bad feeling, I thought. *Should I say something?* I decided against it as I explored the downstairs, still hugging myself tightly. Fifth Street had made me skittish. Gram may have felt this same feeling, but she was so fearless, it wouldn't have deterred her—nothing that a little TV televangelism cranked to ten couldn't fix. Right off the kitchen, where we'd come in through the back door, was a huge room with a dark, open doorway in the far corner. I approached it cautiously and glanced up into a very claustrophobic, narrow servants' staircase. I shuddered: halfway up through the dark, something was glaring at me, I could feel it! I jerked back, telling myself it was only my imagination, and quickly moved into the spacious front room where Mom and Gram were still excitedly making plans.

I followed them up the front staircase, which ended in a tall, tight hallway—so cramped you could touch each wall with arms outstretched. With the bedrooms off to each side behind massive oaken doors, and original gaslights protruding from the walls, it was an impressive specimen of Victorian architecture. The last bedroom at the end of the hall was right beside that servants' staircase that had just given me the heebie-jeebies. I sidestepped fearfully, barely glancing in. It was thick with "something." I could feel it, and I was pretty sure I didn't want to spend much time at Grandma's house.

After Gram got moved in, my mom started the hard work of wallpapering. With fifteen-foot ceilings and so much square footage, it dragged on much longer than they'd imagined. With ladders, wallpaper, and paste trays scattered throughout, the house was a mess. One evening after Mom had left for the day, Grandma sat in her favorite chair and dozed off in front of the TV while watching the evening news.

But something awakened her suddenly, and when she opened her eyes, she saw what it was: a woman—an older lady just standing there between her and the TV. Startled, Grandma jumped, and though she was going deaf, she somehow telepathically understood the woman was upset about the messy state of the house.

"I'm hurrying as fast as I can," Grandma protested, as the woman wrung her hands. She was a handsome woman with graying hair, rather stout, wearing a dark dress with small white polka dots.

As soon as Grandma said these words addressing the visitor's concerns, the woman faded away.

The next day, she told Mom about the incident, and a few days after that, while she was out in the side yard, the next-door neighbor came over to welcome her to the neighborhood. After they introduced themselves, Grandma asked about the previous owners.

"I just happen to have a picture of the lady who lived here," the neighbor said, voice raised enough so Gram could hear her. "Let me run in and get it."

Gazing at the large bay window on the side of the home and all the weeds that had grown up below it, Gram waited. The house even had a "cement pond"; a small fishpond, which Victorians sometimes had on their estates for their amusement.

"Here she is," said the neighbor loudly, presenting Gram with a black and white snapshot.

"Oh my!" Grandma could not think what to say as she looked at the picture from a decade earlier: a stout woman, graying hair swept back in a bun, wearing the exact same dress as she'd worn in her living room a couple days before.

"She passed away not long after this picture was taken," said her neighbor. "She loved your house." Grandma didn't have the heart to tell her she hadn't left it.

The scariest room in the house, the one upstairs beside that narrow servants' staircase, must have had the same effect on Gram as it did on me. She kept it closed off, using it only for storage.

One of Mom's brothers lived in the mansion with Grandma for a while. He would come home from work dirty, and go to the basement to shower. There was a small pile of old bricks scattered near one wall, and he threw them one by one back into a dark crawlspace. The next day, the bricks were stacked neatly in the center of the room. He knew Grandma didn't venture into the basement. He would again throw them into the crawlspace, and every time he took a shower, he would hear the noise of them moving. Again, the next day they'd be neatly stacked. My uncle didn't want to talk about it, and the story was pieced together via cousins from whatever we all could pry out of our parents. Being close-mouthed about these things was a continuing family tradition.

The place was a bit too restless even for Gram, and she soon moved. We heard that a new owner fell (or was she pushed, as she claimed?) down the front staircase, breaking her leg. The house didn't seem to keep owners long. Years later, I returned when I found out my friend Judy's family had moved into the house. It was odd to be in Gram's old home with a whole new set of people and furniture. But one thing was familiar: her mother had her TV and sitting room just as Grandma had hers. I forced myself to follow my friend up those narrow, little, back servants' stairs to her bedroom at the end of that skinny hall, shades of Fifth Street crowding me the whole way. She had the creepiest room in the house and I could still feel it. The room that even totally fearless Gram was overwhelmed by—my friend slept in it every night! I shuddered and tried to make small talk. I didn't stay long, but I asked if she'd had any problems there.

"I hear noises," she said, eyes wide with fear. Then she clammed up. But later, when I saw her out somewhere— away from the house—she told me what had happened.

Judy's parents were devout Catholics and her little sister was making her first communion. After the service, there was a family party back at their house. Of course, Judy's mom wanted a record of her youngest daughter in her communion dress.

"Honey, come here so I can get a picture of you look- ing so pretty," she called. "Stand right there, in front of the TV, and smile." Then she snapped a Polaroid pic- ture, pulled it out of the camera, and waved it dry while Judy and her little sister eagerly waited to see it. As Judy watched, a look of puzzlement then horror came over her mom's face. "No!" screamed her mom, ripping the picture to pieces. And she refused to say more, no matter how much they begged. Judy told me that later her mom had confided that there was a woman in a polka-dotted dress standing behind her little sister.

Not long ago, a new generation moved into the old ghost house. My young cousin found out some friends had moved there. It had been broken up into apartments not too long after Judy's family moved out. My cousin told me about the young guys who shared the upstairs, and the one who'd slept in that very bad room at the end of the hall.

Apparently, he'd constantly accused his roommates of messing with him, coming in his room at night and moving his things. Finally, one morning before they were to take a trip, the kid came down to breakfast saying he'd had no sleep all night, that someone else would have to drive while he slept. He said something had kept him up all night, scratching at the walls, as if trying to get in or get out. Later on, my cousin asked the roommates what had happened, and they told him they'd just moved the boy's room into the basement, turning the bad room upstairs into storage once again. My cousin didn't have the heart to tell them what happened in the basement. That poor kid. Our family still refers to Gram's old house as "the ghost house."

4

After the Storm,
the Flood

That year I landed my first professional music job in an old hotel in Zoar, Ohio. It was beautifully restored, one hundred sixty years old, with winding staircases, cupolas, and a basement bar called the Rathskellar, where I played three nights a week. The beams and hand-hewn stone walls created ambiance much bigger than the bar itself. It even had its own ghost, which I did my best to avoid, though at times I felt strange vibes.

I was still having prophetic dreams and flashes of clairvoyance, but I didn't pay much attention. I was too busy finding myself and trying to forget what I knew. I thought things were finally better. After all, they couldn't get much worse than Fifth Street and a marriage ending. I was in a frenzy to make up for lost time and move my life forward.

One night after my gig at the Rathskellar, I hurried to meet my girlfriends at the dance club where we all hung out. I noticed a guy who stood out like a diamond among coal. Unlike anyone else, he made quite an impression. Extremely good looking, in a sensuous Brad Pitt *Interview with a Vampire* way, he was very well dressed. I'd never seen him around before, or anyone like him, in our little town.

"Who is THAT?" I asked my friends, nodding his way. One of them knew his name, that he was from a neighboring town, and a year older. They told me he drove a sports car.

Of course, I thought. *Bonus!*

Tall and graceful, he had dark hair, a perfect face and body, and a small smile playing on his full, sensuous lips that seemed to say, "I know how good I look; enjoy me." Everyone was watching him, though no one wanted to let on they were. Being somewhat unconventional myself and preferring the beat of a different drum, I was smitten. But I hadn't had a serious guy in my life since my ex, let alone one who looked like this. He was out of my league.

At some point, I was introduced. He was charming and well-spoken, and even more drop-dead gorgeous up close. My theory was you usually got one or the other; beauty or brains. I'd always liked brains, but he was so pretty, it wouldn't have mattered.

I considered myself average looking, while my two best friends were beautiful. I was blessed with the gift of gab, and they were beauties most comfortable staying quiet. They'd sometimes ask me to play "mouthpiece" and talk to guys they were interested in. Guys were always falling all over them.

From the beginning, this gorgeous stranger was different. Ignoring my girlfriends, he concentrated on me. Could he be interested? He came on strong, and I didn't know what to make of it. Ignoring the litany of psychic nudges that something wasn't right, I was bewitched.

"Your friends tell me you're a musician," he said, cocking his head quizzically. "When can I come see you play?"

"Yes, I am," I laughed, trying to keep my voice from rising like a five-year-old's. "I'm playing tomorrow at the Rathskellar. It's a great place."

"I've been there," he said. "Good food."

"Yeah, it is. But I don't think I've ever seen you there," I replied, feigning disinterest.

"No, at least not while *you* were playing. I'd have remembered *you*." His smile produced a small dimple in one cheek and perfectly even white teeth. And stifling every psychic nudge and shove, I decided then and there that I needed this man as a boyfriend...even if it meant giving up everything I had.

He showed up at the Rathskellar that weekend, and we spent breaks talking and, afterwards, met my friends in town. The more attentive he was, the more grateful I felt.

I squashed the little voice inside that said he was playing me like an instrument. He asked me out, and I went on my first real date since my ex.

We saw each other regularly. He did all the romantic things I'd never known: roses on Sweetest Day, shopping trips to big cities where he bought me clothes, letting me drive his Corvette. I tried hard to be cool enough for him, showing him what I knew about the occult, and performing love spells to bind him to me. I would've done anything to prove I was special and different to be good enough for him. I was so in love that I ignored the red flags. There were a few.

One day after a stop at McDonald's, driving north on the freeway, he suddenly spilled a drop of strawberry milkshake on his clothes—and in a rage instantly threw the cup at the closed passenger window, where I was sitting. It exploded and strawberry milkshake went everywhere. I sat, frozen in shock as milkshake dripped down the window and ran down my hair and clothes. This was a warning that, somehow, I ignored. I figured he'd lost his temper. Since he went back to being sweet as could be, I was appeased and soon even deeper in love.

After about six months, one night while in his car outside the club, he asked me to marry him. *Don't do this*, screamed the little voice inside me.

I told him I'd just gotten out of a marriage that was a mistake, and even though I really wanted to, asked if we could just live together first to see how it went. He wasn't real happy, but he agreed.

The next month was spent finding an apartment, and looking forward to my brand-new life with my new love. I had to fib about Cryer, since pets weren't allowed, but I just couldn't leave her with my folks. I felt so lucky and was hoping I'd soon feel safe enough to say yes to his proposal.

We fell into a routine of domestic tranquility. I loved all the things most people would consider drudgery, like cleaning and cooking. Now that I was so in love, it was fun!

On the weekends I played, he'd come along, and we always made it a party by inviting others. I didn't see my friends much otherwise; this new life isolated me, and he wanted me all to himself.

One night, I was sitting on the sofa, a lighted makeup mirror in front of me on the coffee table. We'd been talking off and on while he was in the other room, nothing important. I remember not agreeing on something small, where to go or that sort of thing. Not in anger, just playfully.

"So, don't we have to make an appearance where the 'in crowd' is tonight?" he said as he walked into the room.

"Oh yeah, right," I replied sarcastically, leaning forward into my mirror. "I don't think anyone would notice either way." And he kicked the mirror into my face, the sharp corner cutting me close to my eye.

I was so shocked. I stood up, holding my eye, staring at him, trying to make sense of this. Was it an accident?

Expressionless, he looked at me, and then walked away. *Oh my God*, I thought. *He did it on purpose.*

Cut, black-eyed, and traumatized, I told myself maybe I deserved it. After all, my mom always said I was "mouthy." Over and over, I replayed the incident, trying to understand *why*. I *was* being sarcastic. Maybe he didn't mean to actually kick it into my *face*; maybe *that* part was an accident. This wasn't the guy I knew! After Fifth Street, I suddenly wondered which was scarier—the known or the unknown?

For a while, he'd always seemed mad about something, often getting angry that I didn't like the same things he liked. I'd also come to realize he wasn't fond of intellectual things, and he felt inferior if I mentioned a word he didn't know. But I wasn't about to lobotomize myself for anyone, not even him.

Instead I'd forgive him. After all, I wasn't sure who was to blame—and anyone could lose their temper once. I loved him, he was so beautiful, and I felt so lucky to have him. It all made sense: I'd come through hell to get to this point, and I'd finally found the good things I deserved. I had a music career, a beautiful apartment, and a beautiful man who'd worked hard to make me fall in love with him. I would forgive him and we'd move on.

Things went smoothly for a while and I almost forgot what had happened. My parents had taught me that anything I wanted was possible to achieve, just by believing I could do it. I thought if I did my part, made a nice home, cooked, cleaned, made money, became everything to everybody, how could it not work? I'd always been a peacekeeper, a mediator, the one who tried to "fix" everything.

But I began to notice a constant between us: there was always one "mad" and one trying to "make up." Nothing was mutual—it was always lopsided. And it was exhausting. Still, I continued to try to please him…and over and over I saw his naked pleasure in rejecting my efforts.

The next incident was bad. Who knows what set him off, but suddenly he was screaming right up in my face, scaring me to death. I put my arms straight out to stop him from coming any closer, and he went ballistic. Reaching through my arms, he grabbed my hair and started screaming—just indecipherable insane screaming—his rage going from zero to a hundred in a split second. I'd never experienced anything even remotely like this; my parents never even argued! He dragged me by the hair through the entire apartment—living room, dining room, and finally into the bedroom, where he threw me onto the bed and tried to sit on me.

I flailed to keep him away and hit him in the eye. Yanking me flat on my back, he pinned me down. He was over six feet tall and 200 pounds, and I was 120. I couldn't move. I could only watch as he drew back his fist and punched me.

I don't remember too much after that. My eye hurt. My head was on fire from being dragged by the hair. I was seeing stars as I felt him get off me, and then I heard him leaving the room.

"You gave me a black eye," he screamed from the bathroom. The back door slammed, and he was gone.

He barely had a mark on his eye, but I had to stay out of sight for several weeks while mine healed. My parents' instruction that I could do anything if I believed in myself may have resulted in the confusion and denial that had kept me in this relationship so far, but it also had a benefit. I *knew* I deserved better than this, and that something was terribly wrong with this man.

He was so sorry when he returned. Although I wanted to believe him, I could no longer deny that something was really, really wrong. But I knew I had to hide this from him. Love and fear are not a good combination.

My black eye wasn't even completely healed when I found out I was pregnant. I was terrified, scared to tell him, scared not to. Expecting another beating, I delivered the news. "Get rid of it," he sneered, handing me money. "I'm not ready to be a father."

The only thing I know for sure is his violence left me feeling like I had no choice. No one knew, not friends, not family. I was locked into this violent nightmare with him alone. Though I may have been a victim of circumstance and abuse, so was an innocent unborn life. The doctor said something was wrong with it, that I would have miscarried, and I wondered if the last beating somehow caused this. But still, I will always feel the need to atone, and always wonder about the karma involved.

It still took one more violent beating before I truly listened to my clairvoyant "little voice"—the voice that was always on my side. When he attacked me again a month later, as I ran for the safety of the bedroom, Cryer barking frantically at my heels, he grabbed his rifle from the closet, and I heard it: "*Do the best acting job of your life*," it whispered in my head, my left side tingling. And finally I listened.

"Look at us," I said quietly—acting like the rifle pointed at my stomach was of no concern at all. He was hysterical, sobbing and screaming, and I knew he could easily kill me. "What's happened to us?" I asked. He seemed to calm down a little. "Can't we go back to what we used to be?" I pleaded softly. He started to cry with the self-pity I'd seen before. No matter how bad he treated me, somehow he felt like *he* was a victim. I could never figure this out.

He laid the gun down, and I walked to him and embraced him, still talking softly, as if to a child or dangerous animal. I knew deep inside that he'd probably kill me next time.

Somehow I got through the night, and early in the morning when he left for work, I called a friend, loaded my stuff, and moved back to my parents' house.

Once again, I thought the worst had happened. And once again, I was wrong. Reeling from the sudden loss of everything important in my life, I fell into a depression over what I'd done and what I'd been through. I loved him, and couldn't understand what happened, why he couldn't act like he had in the beginning.

I fell into a dark place, drank to excess, and took whatever drugs that were offered me—the more mind-numbing the better. I went to a concert one night alone; my friends had canceled. I was at overdose levels and can't even remember the concert or anything afterward either. A true blackout.

The next day I woke up in a strange house; anything could have happened and probably did. All I felt was more shame on top of shame. It was all my fault.

I went to the doctor. I couldn't sleep, I told him, and wanted pills. That night, while driving around, I let it all come flooding in: Fifth Street, a marriage, a divorce, a new "true" love, violent abuse, the loss of a baby and a dream, and now the shame of this new incident. I bought a Coke, opened the pills, and took a handful.

As the pills begin to take effect, the familiar little voice inside spoke to me, and maybe it *is* the voice of God that resides inside us all. It told me of my worth, that I wasn't to blame for these terrible things, and that my life would get better. I barely made it to the home of a friend, who took me to the hospital. I woke having my stomach pumped.

I was too ashamed to tell anyone what had prompted this suicide attempt. The friend who'd taken me to the hospital was a musician too—and we were both products of the drug culture. I simply told him I took too many pills. He already knew I'd been going to extremes lately. But I still blamed myself for it all. I was forced to see a psychiatrist for a while, and I didn't even tell *him* what happened. I thought I would take it all to my grave. It was twenty years before I finally told another friend the truth. By then, society was a bit more enlightened; domestic violence, rape, codependence, addictive personalities, and all the other hot topics had come and gone and educated us all.

The first night I ventured out, very fragile after my overdose, I saw my abuser at a club. He watched me condescendingly, a big smirk on his face. I held my head up, but felt like dying inside. I needed something to happen, to change my direction, or I just wasn't going to make it. And in another "coincidence," the next day I got the call that finally changed my life.

5

Small Town Girl Meets World

Earlier that summer, I'd met a guy who was in a local friend's band. Their band was now based in New York. I brought the keyboard player, Rod, to my gig one night so he'd have something to do while our mutual friend attended a family function. Rod seemed like a nice guy, and of course was a musician, which gave us a lot in common.

We made small talk on my breaks and I dropped him off at my friend's house late that night. The band left town the next day, and I didn't give it another thought.

During the next months, as I went through my personal drama, Rod's band was breaking up.

"So, how do you feel about joining my new band?" he asked as soon as I answered the phone. "We have a few good players already. I think you'd round things out nicely. We'd be very versatile."

The thought of leaving all I knew frightened me, but I recognized that a change of scenery was necessary if I was ever going to get over what happened. My self-esteem was in the toilet, but the little voice said *go,* and I had a brief flash of hope.

I drove to Columbus to meet them, jam, and see if we could put this new band together. Mom watched Cryer for me, and I'd get home to see her whenever I could. Though I wanted to turn the car around the whole way there, I kept driving, swallowed my fears, and listened to the little voice.

Our first guitar player's family was an interesting one; his dad was a pioneer of early "Big Time" wrestling, and his sister was the last wife of Dr. Sam Sheppard, whose murder trial made F. Lee Baily famous as well as spawned *The Fugitive* series and movies. Every time I walked into his mom's kitchen and stepped over the spot where he told me Dr. Sam collapsed and died, I shuddered. I could still feel the vibe there, and the history.

I was still shy and traumatized over recent events, but none of these new friends knew what I'd gone through. The band gave me a renewed sense of purpose, a fresh outlook, and talented friends who respected me. It was all good, finally. I was so glad I hadn't turned the car around.

Along with all this new happiness, I found that my psychic streak was heightened; it got even stronger after the overdose.

Our band's first road trip to Terre Haute, Indiana, was exciting. The Ramada Inn, with its big white pillars and grand looking entrance, seemed like Heaven's Gates. So far, I loved the road!

One night I happened to mention my haunted house experience to a waitress at the Ramada restaurant, letting slip that I was psychic. The word got out and it turned into a free-for-all of the staff wanting readings, which escalated into readings on my breaks—for customers as well. Once someone sees a tarot spread being laid or a palm reading in progress, they flock around and want to be next. It's always been this way. This alone could've become a full-time job and sometimes I had to turn people away to play. I was too afraid to charge; I still thought of it as a hobby, but I accepted tips, and it supplemented my income.

The waitresses told me about a strange old woman they'd been to, a psychic, but they called her a witch. She was temperamental, and if she didn't like your looks or got some bad vibes, she'd turn you away. They spoke of her in hushed tones in fear of her abilities and the knowledge she had about their lives that she couldn't possibly have known, but somehow did. Immediately I begged for directions to her house.

———

As I picked my way through dark, narrow alleyways in a seedy section of town, I almost changed my mind. Twisted old trees cast spooky shadows as they hovered over the small houses on the street, some not much more than shacks. Her house was tiny and dark, and I made my way onto a rickety porch and tentatively knocked on the door. A mangy cat slunk away around the corner with a fearful backward glance at me. *Black cat, how cliché,* I thought.

An old woman with deep-set eyes and a halo of frizzy, white hair enveloping her head and framing her face opened the door a crack and peered out at me, a sour, acrid smell seeping out around her.

"What do you want?" she asked softly.

"Ma'am, I'm not from around here. I was told you could tell me about my future," I said.

"What do you wanna know that for?" she answered with a cackle. "You're just borrowing trouble. Sufficient unto the day is the evil thereof." I smiled back, remembering all the times my mom and grandma had said the same thing, quoting the Bible.

"I guess I have an interest in what you have to say," I told her. "I'm only in town for a little while, and some girls who came to you told me about you."

She paused, thoughtfully looking me up and down, then slowly opened the door. I followed her into the small, dark room, where she pointed to one of two straight-backed chairs at a round, wooden table. I didn't see a single chicken foot or voodoo doll anywhere, and I relaxed, trying not to wrinkle my nose at the odor. We both sat, her eyes never leaving my face. Not wanting to breathe the strange smell in, I held my breath as long as I could.

"Let me see your hand," she said. I stretched out my palm toward her and she held it in her own wrinkled hands, finally breaking her gaze and concentrating on what she saw there. "You will have much to give, and will give joy to many, a very public life," she said, tracing the lines on my palm with one gnarled finger. "But you yourself will stop short of all you dream, as you are destined to seek, but never find."

I thought this was a very sad pronouncement. I didn't believe it for one minute; I was young, ambitious, and had plans to be a rock star.

"If you do not die at age thirty-six, you will live to ninety-three," she continued, "but darkness follows you, my dear, and you will do well to stay close to God."

"What do you mean by darkness?" I asked. *Could it be from Fifth Street?* I wondered. "And what will happen at age thirty-six?" I was barely twenty-one, so it seemed very far away.

"Some things only God knows," she answered, dropping my hand. "There are voices that speak without words. God speaks to you; listen."

She sat quietly, looking quizzically at me, and I was afraid to ask her any more, a bad feeling coming over me. I stood up in a rush, noisily scraping the chair legs against the floor, thanked her, and laid ten dollars on the table. I felt a little faint as I made my way to the door. I looked back and she still sat where I'd left her. I barely whispered a goodbye and turned to go.

"Sorrow is the pathway to God," she pronounced, as I stepped out onto the porch, the smell of her house stuck in my nostrils. *What the hell was that all about?* I thought. I quickly ran to my car. I wanted to get away as fast as I could; this hadn't been much fun at all. *Sorrow the pathway to God? Sheesh!*

I thought about the witch and what she said for a long time afterwards. Was I attracting the dark energy, or somehow creating it? Was she just a crazy old woman, or could it have followed me from Fifth Street? I believed only God knew when someone would die, and *I* surely wouldn't ever predict such a thing in *my* readings. I wondered if all the strange and negative incidents in my life so far had been some kind of test. I'd always searched for meaning behind things; but maybe they were just random events. Now all these new temptations on the road were starting. "Behold I send you forth as sheep in the midst of wolves," jumped into my mind. I didn't know the answers yet, but one thing I did know: I'd stopped believing in coincidences after Fifth Street.

6

Sex, Drugs, Rock 'n' Roll

We traveled all over the United States, from Iowa to Alabama, North Carolina to Michigan, Arkansas to Indiana, Illinois and our home state of Ohio. That translates to lots of nightclubs, hotels, and performances. Before long, I was a seasoned veteran.

Other than the readings I did for patrons or employees, I was too busy with music to focus much on psychic gifts. They were still there, and used to some extent, but for the most part, I tried to ignore them. Unless, of course, they were warning me about something—then they were impossible to ignore. This happened a few times, and several incidents were fairly traumatic. Trauma reinforced the need for psychic abilities, while it simultaneously honed them. I was getting good at recognizing the warnings, even if not quite ready to listen.

One night after a gig in Indianapolis, we went to Denny's for breakfast. The restaurant was packed, and all six of us stood in the foyer waiting for a table. Along the wall to the left was a row of padded benches with tables. I looked in that direction and saw a man, drunk or high, nodding off over his plate. A harmless junkie.

My psychic antennae gave a little jolt, a feeling of danger, but I often got this upon entering a situation with a lot of people. It was hard to pinpoint exactly what it meant or where it was coming from. As I scanned the room to make sense of it, the junkie started talking to our guitar player.

"No thanks, man," I heard our guitar player say. "We're waiting on a table big enough for us all."

"What did he want?" I asked when he turned back to me.

"Oh, he just asked if I wanted to sit with him," he answered, rolling his eyes.

The junkie was directly behind us now, as we'd turned to face the crowded restaurant. Fifteen minutes went by, and I kept feeling something wrong, but I also felt watched by all the diners. Maybe this was making me uncomfortable, so I kept pushing the danger feeling down. As the waitress came for us, she looked worried. She seated us, telling us what happened.

"Oh my God," she began—

CRASH—the police suddenly burst in, guns drawn. "ON THE FLOOR," they screamed, grabbing the junkie and dragging him out the doors. Seated almost directly across from this, we had a perfect view. They beat him with nightsticks until his shoes flew off.

"What in the world…" I began.

"What did you say to him?" The waitress asked.

"Nothing," I answered. "He asked our guitar player to sit there, and he said no thanks."

"Well, he's been aiming a gun at your heads for fifteen minutes," she replied. "Didn't you know it?"

One look at my white face should have told her we *didn't* know it! I couldn't eat and just wanted to get out of there. I knew better than to ignore that feeling, but I still kept trying to pretend I didn't have it.

A slightly different version was repeated in another city, when a disgruntled patron started firing shots at his cheating girlfriend, who happened to be directly in line with the stage. As the bullets whizzed by and the ducking commenced, I told myself this wasn't what I signed up for. Once again, something had felt wrong before it started, and again, I'd ignored it.

Another time, we were hired to play a wedding reception at the club where we were booked for the week. The reception was during the day, and they were a rough-looking bunch, but it was extra money. All was well until after it was over and most guests had left. A few family members were cleaning up the food tables as I made my way to the restroom. The guys in the band were in the dressing room, so there was no one around. I started to get a very bad feeling, but I couldn't figure out why. There was literally nobody around.

I stepped into the restroom, and instead of going to a stall, I stood puzzled, looking into the large mirror above the sinks, trying to sort out where the feeling was coming from. I dabbed at my eye makeup with a paper towel as I opened myself to the feeling.

Suddenly the door opened, and I watched in the mirror as two very large men came in behind me and stood stock still, shoulder to shoulder, blocking the door, and staring at me, expressionless. My heart jumped into my throat, all my instincts and abilities screaming that they'd come to rape me. *This* was the danger. I remained completely calm somehow, casually moving only my eyes back to my own image in the mirror, my hand up to my eye wiping makeup. *BE STRONG*, shouted the voice inside my head. It took all my courage to say sarcastically, "I think you've got the wrong restroom, boys." Then I nonchalantly gathered my makeup bag, coolly tossed the paper towel, and forced myself to walk toward them as they blocked the door. At the last second they parted, allowing me through, apparently thinking twice about what they'd had in mind when I didn't seem scared or weak.

When I got back to the band room, I went ballistic. Screaming, ranting, and raving out of fear, and rage. It brought back memories of what had happened to me,

when I'd determined I'd never be a victim again. It took
the guys a while to get the story out of me, and by that
time, the men were long gone. The guys did tell the club
owner, but nothing could've been done, since the threat
was in my own mind only. The men could simply say
they'd come into the wrong restroom. But I knew better.

Sometimes it was hard to decipher the feelings, and
though I was learning to listen to them, there were times
they didn't work like I wished. But then again, they never
did work very well when I wanted them to help me in any
slightly selfish way, like winning money or spotting a good
opportunity.

We'd had trouble finding the perfect lead guitar player
during this phase of the band. Some guitar players had a
good work ethic and less talent; others, no work ethic
with massive talent. Our guitar player at that time was
of the massive-talent variety, with one foot in and one
foot out of the band. Once again, he'd given a two-week
notice to leave. A music magazine writer we'd befriended
heard about our search and said she had a younger guy
who was perfect for us. Thrilled, we invited them up to
the band house in Michigan, hoping for a talented, com-
patible player.

We were all relaxing after the gig when there was a
knock at the downstairs door.

"Come on in," I yelled down the stairs, "it's open."
From the top of the staircase, I watched as a pretty young

man bounded up. He had long, straight blond hair past his shoulders.

We settled down to talk and get a feel for his personality. We hoped we could work him right into the band, because every week we didn't play was a week without income.

Billy certainly looked like a rock star, which was important—looks were part of the whole package that our audiences expected. I was hoping he'd have the talent to back it up. We talked into the early morning hours, until finally, we all started drifting off to bed. The plan was to audition Billy the next day.

At the crack of noon, we piled into the van and headed to the club downtown. Onstage, Billy soloed in the correct spot, his timing was good. When he sang some backups, his voice was unique and different. But then, we didn't need a vocalist. We needed a great lead guitar player, and he just wasn't the caliber of player we needed. With a smile pasted on my face, my heart sank. I hated this part. Plus I liked him now! He was extremely sexy and eager to please. We all recognized he just wasn't good enough yet. Most likely he would be eventually, but he was so young, it would take a few years.

The guys all gathered around and thanked him again, and I told him we'd call as soon as we made a decision.

As he left the club, we looked at each other dejectedly. He wasn't the one. Eventually our guitar player decided to stay, and we entered the last phase of the band's existence.

A few years later, after we'd gotten off the road, I saw Billy Bailey again. I was watching MTV. I loved the song playing and thought the singer looked familiar. On closer look, it was Billy! Cuter than ever in leather pants and big hair, he grasped the microphone, doing some sexy serpentine moves. He'd moved to California a couple years after our audition, changed his name to Axl Rose, and started a band called Guns N' Roses. The rest is history. I wish my clairvoyance would've told me to hire him!

———

As I ran from my past toward my dream of becoming a rock star, I looked back at the journey that'd brought me to this point. I was on the road with a top band, playing fifty weeks a year, making good money, writing and recording songs in state-of-the-art studios, and finally getting notice from record companies. It'd been four years of hard work, and I knew it was only a matter of time until I achieved my dream. I wouldn't have quit until I did…except for more darkness.

I was twenty-four years and five months old, and we were in Ann Arbor, when I got a bad toothache. I made it all week, then drove home to the dentist. An abscessed wisdom tooth, he said, and he needed to pull it. I canceled the following week to get it done.

Glad to have the tooth out, I was looking forward to time off with family and snuggling Cryer. But the next morning, I was awakened very early with an excruciating pain in my left shoulder—the same side as the tooth extraction.

In agony, I thought I somehow broke my shoulder in my sleep! Mom called our doctor and he got me in that day. He listened, took blood, and mentioned, under his breath, that he "hoped it wasn't arthritis."

My experience was a dramatic introduction to the disease. It didn't take me long to research the symptoms and self-diagnose, but it took a year for the blood tests to officially reveal Rheumatoid Arthritis.

The following year was spent trying to stop it or slow it down while continuing my life: recording our first album, performing on stages across the country, and trying to salvage my dream. Rod and I had slowly become more than friends, and we got married the summer after I developed the R.A. By the time the band disintegrated the following May, I was barely able to lift my leg to climb onto a stage.

I tried experimental medicines, and every treatment I could find, but nothing worked. Ever since I was seven, I'd told anyone who'd listen that I'd be a famous singer. How I hated and feared the death of that dream.

Down to the bitter end, that last month on the road, I still had hopes: maybe I'd respond to treatment; maybe then I could still succeed in the music business. My deterioration was obvious to everyone but me, and

I lamely struggled on. "Never give up," had always been my motto.

The week before I threw in the towel, we were booked in southern Ohio. It was a slow night. We'd finished our second set, and I made my way to the restroom. I walked by empty tables, changed course to talk to the bartender—exchanging brief pleasantries about how slow it was—then backtracked to the restroom. All the tables had been empty, but suddenly, abruptly, without my seeing anybody enter the club, there was a guy at the table in front of me. He stared at me oddly and I gave him a brief nod and a half smile as I walked past, a weird feeling coming over me.

"Miss, can I speak with you?" he asked in a formal way, very out of place in a rock club.

"Sure," I replied wearily. I was in pain and exhausted from lack of sleep and the effects of experimental medicines. "I'll be right out." I gave him a weak smile and made my way to the restroom, where I looked at my reflection in the mirror: I was skin and bones, with deep purple shadows under my eyes; all big hair and bony angles from a twenty-pound weight loss I could hardly afford. I rubbed my swollen hands, bright red at the knuckles, and looked into my own sad eyes—the face of defeat. It was over. I was very sick and very scared.

Then, with a big sigh and "show must go on" mentality, I returned to the club, pasted on the brightest smile I could manage, and tried not to limp as I made my way to the man with the formal speech.

He had dark blond hair and was physically very average. I couldn't tell you what he wore; everything about him was nondescript. Except his eyes. The strangest eyes I've ever seen; pale blue—the lightest blue, unearthly. He stared at me, expressionless, until I felt uncomfortable.

"I didn't see you come in," I stammered, making small talk. "It's kind of slow tonight."

The young man continued to study me. I felt funny. I wanted to get up and leave, but because this was so different from what normally transpired with fans, I forced myself to act as though everything was normal—as I always do when something's wrong.

"Do you believe what you're doing is God's will?" he suddenly asked. "Do you feel you are misusing your gift from God?"

I could not have been more thunderstruck! Because, in fact, I *did* very much feel that way. The sicker I got, the closer I'd become to God, questioning everything that happened, praying for healing, hoping to find a way to continue...and yet wondering if singing "Highway to Hell" on a nightly basis was really why God gave me this voice. Somehow, he knew.

"It's funny you should ask this, because I've always worried about this very thing," I nearly whispered, dumbfounded. The shock I felt at his question didn't give me time to wonder at the strangeness, the inappropriateness of it. Frozen in place, unable to get up and end this, something simultaneously fascinated and repelled me, like a mouse in the sights of a cobra. Those pale blue, unblinking eyes watched me coolly, unemotionally, seemingly weighing something, gathering evidence, making a judgment.

"I feel God gave me this talent and I've always abused it; used it for gain or to seek fame. I'm not sure if this is what He really wanted for me or if it's just what *I* wanted," I told him, wondering why I was confessing this to a stranger, and a scary one at that. But I was compelled; it was like he knew me, like I knew him—from somewhere, sometime that I couldn't quite remember. I've never felt this way since. The silence stretched out between us.

"Only you can decide," he finally said, the gaze from those strange blue eyes unwavering. "Only you. We all make choices, we all must decide, and live with what we choose," he continued. "You must decide." Unmoving, unblinking, he sat there.

Suddenly overcome with fear, I pulled free of his will and slowly stood, our eyes still locked. I somehow broke our gaze and looked toward the stage at the guys gathering there. Break was over.

"I have to go," I said backing away.

He continued to stare at me, and I felt the pull of his strangeness as I forced myself to turn my back on him and walk to the stage. Deeply worried, feeling my psychic voice warning me about something, I turned to look back at him as I reached the stage, and he was gone. Just gone. Not there anymore. I looked toward the exit. No one.

In shock, I went across the stage to Rod to try to explain what had just happened. Actually, not much *had* happened. But the awful feeling it generated, the residual effect it had on me, that's what I tried to explain for the rest of the night.

How did he slip out like that, so fast? It was impossible. How? For that matter, how did he arrive there the same way? This scared me deeply; I felt he was a messenger of some sort, but if I had to choose from which side, I couldn't have. Was he an angel trying to show me another path? Was he a demon disgusted with my loyalty to God even under such adverse conditions? Was he trying to explain the concept of "free will" to me? Or was he just a weird guy with his own psychic streak, needing answers to some moral dilemma? I felt crazy trying to explain. Thankfully Rod had seen me sitting with him, so I knew it'd really happened, that I hadn't somehow hallucinated it. What did he mean by I had to *decide*? Decide what? Whether I wanted to stay on the road, serve God a little better, or what? I couldn't sleep that night.

I struggled on, still in the game or so I thought, when one day, the band members approached Rod to say they were leaving. A couple had joined other bands. It seemed the height of cruelty and disloyalty to me, as sick as I was. I'd always been so loyal to them, turning down some good offers, but in hindsight I guess it was self-preservation on their parts. Rheumatoid Arthritis seemed to be the only thing that could finally curb my ambition. I told Rod I wouldn't hold him to his promises either, but Rod was also loyal to a fault, so together we moved into our new lives, in the real world.

7

You CAN Go Home Again

We returned to my hometown and moved in with my parents until Rod found a job. In some ways, I was relieved to leave what had become an untenable position: I was so sick, yet had felt responsible for five other band members' jobs.

When I'd developed the arthritis, doctors advised against having children because of the medications and physical difficulties. But I wanted to be a mom badly, so I had to take the chance.

When I was two months along, I dreamt it was a boy and I'd have a Caesarean section. This scared me, but I convinced myself it was "just a dream"—my way of coping;

in those days, I felt saner and less fearful if I shrugged off information that came through dreams, or clairvoyance.

In childbirth classes, the instructor said statistics suggested one of us would have a C-section, but since percentages are always about others, I pushed down my fear over the dream.

But when the time came, as I'd dreamed, it was an emergency C-section. A hundred years earlier, we both would've been a different statistic.

James was such an easy baby, always so happy! It was as though he knew he'd been carefully planned and loved from the moment he came into being. Right after he was born, we went shopping for our home. As the realtor guided us through the one we eventually bought, I tried to sniff out any unseen occupants. I knew it might be a strange question, but had to ask if any violent deaths were associated with the property. I explained I'd lived in a haunted house as a girl, and would like to avoid that ever happening again! Homes with violent histories are called "stigmatized property" by realtors. The realtor denied anything of the sort, which calmed my fears.

As I walked from room to room, opening myself, I finally relaxed. This house had a good feel, a warm comforting ambience. When I'm in the presence of a spirit, I usually get a heaviness in my chest and have difficulty breathing, accompanied by a tingling feeling. I didn't get that here. It felt normal.

It was a big four-bedroom home built in 1917 with art nouveau touches throughout. On a busy street, the house had lots of character; beautiful woodwork, pillars, pocket doors, stained and leaded glass, and a walk-up attic. It was a great place for our little family, and the price was right. And there was a grade school a half block down, where I pictured James going to school.

When James was six weeks old, we moved in—a logistical nightmare with me still recovering and dealing with the recurrence of the R.A.—but somehow we pulled it off. James grew and thrived. *Perfect baby, perfect house, perfect life!* I thought.

Not long after moving in, I began "misplacing" things, mostly diaper rash ointment, toys, and whatnot. They disappeared from where I knew I'd left them. So I began experimenting, taking note of where I set things down. I quickly realized I wasn't being forgetful—something was taking things, moving them to other spots! This was puzzling, but not yet frightening, since I only half allowed myself to believe it. Mostly I tried not to think about it, distracted by my exhaustion. I fell into bed and slept until morning, when the new-baby routine started all over again.

When Jamie (his nickname) was a few months old, he began to stare at a spot near the ceiling above his crib, laughing and giggling. Something was really interesting to him up there! I tried to "open" myself a bit, but I couldn't feel anything bad, just a slight energy in the room. *That's just the way babies act*, I told myself, though I'd never been around many.

Rod's mom and dad had passed away within four months of each other a couple years earlier. They'd wanted their only son to have children, but Rod and I were living rock-star lives on the road. *Maybe they're peeking in on their new grandson*, I thought.

This explanation comforted me, as Jamie continued to stare and giggle, and the spooky incidents kept occurring.

Jamie was a precocious baby, saying "doggy" (or "go-ggy") at seven months as he noticed Cryer one day. At fourteen months, he was talking quite a bit, and things heated up, psychically speaking! One night in his room, while rocking him by the light that seeped in from the hallway, it was dark and quiet, but a chill was in the air. "Who dat man?" blurted James in his baby voice, chubby little hand pointing toward the hall.

I froze, because I'd seen a dark shadow move but ignored it, as I'd been doing for a while. Filled with that old familiar fear and dread, I finally admitted there was something else in the house. Something that was attracted to us or to this precious new life I'd have died to protect! *Maybe "the darkness" followed me here too*, I thought, remembering the old witch's words.

In the nursery, I began to get a bad feeling of something right behind me, and I'd jerk around to see who it was. Of course, nothing was ever there. I was worried that James was a focus for this something's attention. Babies often attract this from spirits, and after all, this was an old house. Just to be on the safe side, I moved him into another room, one that felt lighter. I hoped this would quiet things down a little in case the room had a resident other than James.

I'd had my beloved old dog Cryer since I'd found her in Las Vegas at age seventeen. A small, black, part Peking-ese, she'd been through everything with me; Fifth Street, California, and my first marriage; the abusive partner, the road, and now this new phase of my life. She was fourteen and couldn't walk, but wasn't in pain, so I couldn't put her down. I had to carry her out to do her business, but I didn't mind. I couldn't imagine life without her.

One day, as workers finished insulating the house, I ran to the quickie mart three blocks down. I'd carried Cryer outside and sat her in the grass, knowing she'd be okay for five minutes; her back legs were paralyzed. It was almost dusk on a warm spring day.

I bought milk and rushed back, looking to my left at the new plugs in the siding as I slowly drove up the driveway and—bump, bump—both sets of wheels ran over something. I screamed as I realized what had happened. *Oh dear God, somehow Cryer dragged herself over to the driveway!* But how? She couldn't walk at all. Was she trying to watch for me? How did she get there?

I threw it into park and jumped out, hoping beyond hope, and terrified at what I'd see. There, behind my rear wheels, lay Cryer on her side, whimpering softly. I screamed and ran to get Rod, but by the time he came, she was gone.

For days I was inconsolable, unable to stop crying, unable to understand how she got there; Rod hadn't moved her. Thank God I had baby James to distract me. It was the end of an era for me, and I felt cursed for having caused her death. The grief was bad enough, but the fear of being too often singled out by evil was bothering me too. To ease the loss, we found a German shepherd puppy.

Rod's job has always involved the occasional midnight shift. I spent nights alone, with only the new puppy downstairs and baby James in the other room. One night I woke suddenly with the covers pulled down to my ankles. Grabbing the phone, I dialed frantically. "Mom, something pulled my covers off!" I stage whispered, scared something was listening.

"What?" she answered groggily. "You mean something invisible?"

"YES," I shouted, forgetting to keep my voice down. "Can I come down with Jamie?"

"Sure," she answered. "Use your key. You can sleep in your old room."

The rational part of me thought maybe I pushed the covers down in my sleep, though I'd never done that. Plus, I sort of recalled them sliding down as I was starting to wake up. But the part of me that remembered living through Fifth Street expected the worst.

Ever since James had seen the man in the hallway, my senses had been on high alert. It was strange how my acknowledgement and fear seemed to heighten the phenomena, like it was feeding off fear and energy, which was a typical poltergeist response.

One early morning, I was sleeping with my right arm hanging over the side of the bed. As I moved up through layers of sleep, I felt an ice-cold hand tightly grasping my arm in what we called an Indian handshake, where each person grasps the other's wrist, interlocking arms. As I became aware of what was happening, I jerked my arm away in horror. Someone would have to be lying on the floor right beside my bed to do this! When I peeked over, no one was there. *The stuff of childhood nightmares*, I thought, *the monster under the bed!*

With my anxiety escalating, I decided to go through the entire house with a candle, reciting the Lord's Prayer and making a small request of my ghost(s).

"I understand this may have been your house," I began, "but it's our house now. We love it as much as you did. I only ask that you stay in the attic, so we don't see or hear you, and aren't scared by you when we least expect it."

I knew the house felt clean when the realtor showed it, but now, somehow, it seemed as though spirits had found me again. As I said these words, a hush seemed to fall over the house, and I felt a pressure in my ears—like a drop in the barometer before a storm or when your car descends a hill too fast. There was a sense of expectancy, almost like the house was listening. The heaviness in my chest was like someone sitting on me and the tingle up and down my left side went wild—psychic info coming in.

"If you can do this," I continued, "we should be able to live here together peacefully."

After that, things remained fairly quiet in the house, with nothing more than the odd missing item or random feeling or noise. I tried to relax and focus on other things, including family. James was growing up fast, full of energy and becoming a sturdy, smart, and pleasant little boy. I didn't ever want him to know these things went on. My dream was for him to grow up feeling safe and secure, in just one happy home, unlike my sad, fearful childhood.

Soon a strange thing began to happen anytime we returned home and opened the backdoor. We'd no sooner get in the house when one of the heavy oak doors upstairs slammed shut. We always left all four of the upstairs doors open, but the attic door closed. We experimented to see if a draft from opening the backdoor could pull one of the upstairs doors shut, but we couldn't replicate it. Yet we'd hear the slam, check upstairs, and find the doors open as we'd left them, and the attic door closed. *Maybe our ghosts took my suggestion seriously*, I thought, *running into the attic whenever we come home, slamming the door behind them!*

One day James was sitting beside me, quietly playing with a little truck while I was reading a book about the Gold Rush. Stopped at a passage I didn't quite understand, I reread it silently a couple of times. "San Fa-sisco," piped up James in his baby voice. The sentence I was re-reading ended with "San Francisco." I hadn't said anything out loud, not even under my breath, only reading it in my mind. A feeling of awe and disbelief washed over me as I realized that James, too, would be dealing with psychic abilities—and maybe that's why other things were happening in the house.

About this time, a friend came to house-sit while we took a trip. I'll never forget his face the day we got home.

"Mark, what's wrong?" I asked, spotting his worried look when he opened the door. "Is the dog okay?"

"The dog's fine," he replied, looking over his shoulder at the house. "It's me who's not so good!"

"Oh no," I said. "Are you sick?" He sure had a sick look on his face!

"No, not exactly." He laughed uneasily. "But I'm glad you're home. Because I don't think the house likes me."

As I followed him in, he glanced warily up the stairs. Mark was a big, strong guy who wasn't afraid of anything.

"What in the world happened!" I asked.

"Well, the noises I kept hearing were bad enough," he said, "but once they started turning off the bathroom lights, that did it for me!"

Apparently, he'd been lathering himself up in the shower, singing at the top of his lungs, when the lights had gone off! At first he thought it was a power outage…but he stepped out to find the light switch in the off position.

It had been switched off. Then it happened a second time. I joked that maybe they didn't like his singing.

I guess something here didn't want a stranger in the house, let alone a singing one, so this pretty much excluded Mark for future house-sitting jobs.

———

After getting off the road, I'd gone through a spiritual quest, searching for answers to all my questions: Why were my music dreams destroyed in one fell swoop? And by a terrible disease that would pretty much guarantee pain on a daily basis, eventually cripple me, and probably cut my life short? Why would God allow this? I questioned, I raged, I went through all the stages of grief over the loss of my health and my lifelong dream. It seemed spiteful, unfair; it seemed like way more than one person's share of bad luck so far in my life.

Mad at God, I dabbled in pagan religions, joining a family witch's coven and practicing Wicca. Casting good spells to benefit mankind, revering the wind and the earth and ancient gods, I focused on creating good things for others. But my childhood teaching still echoed in my head—"*Thou shalt have no other Gods before me.*"

Although I'd made jokes about the singing-hating ghosts, and attic-hiding ghosts, I still feared paranormal things, and try as I might to fit them into my worldview, I couldn't find their place. I think I felt the need to take control of that fear, to feel as though I was in charge of my life and my destiny. This illusion of being in charge worked for a little while; it made me feel strong at my weakest.

I didn't do many readings in this phase of my life, busy as I was searching for answers and raising James. But it wasn't long before my own psychic abilities scared me once again, and I began to feel the need of the protection of God, the God of my childhood. *Stay close to God,*" echoed the old witch's voice in my head.

My cousin Joyce was my co-conspirator in my ongoing psychic experiments. We were more like sisters than cousins. Joyce, an incredibly talented doll artist, joins me in the fascination with the paranormal. Early on, she helped me practice sending and receiving telepathic messages and pictures.

One night while we were trying to influence the fall of dice to make them come up twos, I scared myself badly.

"Okay, c'mon, let's have some snake eyes," I urged, shaking the dice and throwing them on the hardwood floor.

"TWO," shrieked Joyce, clapping her hands.

"Okay, it's working," I said, amazed. "Gimme a two again." I blew on the dice in my clenched hand, then threw them.

"TWO!" Joyce yelled again. "How cool!"

"Okay, let's see how long this can go on," I said. "C'mon, another two." I laughed, and threw the dice.

"TWO," Joyce shouted when she saw them land, literally jumping up and down and ready to go to Vegas.

I was exhilarated at first, and after four or five times in a row, suddenly terrified. I started to get that feeling of dread again. Was it was me doing this or some little invisible demon crouched on the floor manipulating the dice?

My imagination ran wild when this sort of thing happened. I'd give it all up again for a while, cold turkey, and try to understand why I had this and if I should be using it in this way, or at all. It was emotionally exhausting—back and forth, back and forth. No real answers forthcoming. And sometimes when I tried to use the abilities, I couldn't at all. It was mysterious stuff.

But I still didn't understand God or the big picture any more than anyone does. All I knew for sure was that faith alone is all we're expected to have. I called a tentative truce with Him, pacified somewhat by the gift of James, and life went on.

————

Eventually James started school down the block. Even though he was an only child, and somewhat spoiled by all of us, he was a great little boy who was loving and generous with others. His friends came here to play in the backyard, and there was always a lot of noise and laughter. I loved knowing James was happy and safe at home. I loved being his mother, being engrossed in his life and childhood. I enjoyed it all and focused on him.

But the year I turned thirty-six I lived in fear. According to the witch's prediction all those years before, this could be the year of my death. I didn't want to leave a six-year-old without a mother. I took extra care of my health and was cautious in all areas of life.

One night, near the end of my thirty-sixth year, I had to pick up a friend who was out of town. Driving in unfamiliar territory on a busy, narrow two-lane road, I headed home with James asleep in the back, and my friend in the passenger seat. It was a Friday night and traffic was heavy, a steady line moving fast at fifty-five mph, the headlights of approaching cars making it difficult to see. On my right side, the road was a steep bank, a twenty-foot drop lined with telephone poles: nowhere to go but down.

As I squinted into the oncoming headlights, I saw headlights up ahead pull into my lane to pass. But there wasn't room to pass! As the headlights came straight at us, thinking *this is when the witch's prediction comes true,* I swerved right as far as I could without going over the edge, and at the last second, squeezing my eyes shut, I called out to God. Horns blared as the car flew between us at seventy mph, missing us by a fraction of an inch. Shaken, I pulled over and let my friend drive. Something had saved me. Soon after, I celebrated my thirty-seventh birthday…and the joy of being alive.

———

Rod and I soldiered on, though we'd hit a few rough patches after his parents died and James was born. The loss of parents and becoming a parent can change a man, and we separated for two years when I found out he was seeing someone at work. He wasn't too sure of what he wanted from life. This devastated me, since we'd always been on the same page. After a couple years, he found himself, but then I spent plenty of time getting even. I couldn't get over the betrayal.

It took a couple years of therapy to figure out what was behind my compulsive behaviors: fear and shame. Therapy also led to a diagnosis of post-traumatic stress disorder, and I wondered if psychic abilities were mimicking that condition. Luckily, James was surrounded with love and didn't seem to notice his parents' problems. Eventually, Rod and I became best friends again.

———

Though I was hesitant to let James play in the attic after I'd banished the spirits there, eventually he talked me into it. I'd never told him why I didn't want him up there. He'd sneaked up there often as a boy with no problems, so I finally relaxed a little.

One night when James was seven, he came to me looking scared and wanting to talk about something.

"Mom, I saw people in the front room," he said, eyes big with shock. "They were standing around a coffin with a guy in it. It was sitting on two wooden things holding it up, sort of like Dad's sawhorses."

I questioned him, and he gave a pretty detailed description of what sounded like an old-fashioned wake. In the early days of our house, it's likely that there'd been a viewing of a deceased occupant in the front parlor. The couple that built the home died here, and home wakes were the norm. We could never figure out why our front door was so wide until a history buff told us that it was called a "coffin door," because it was wide enough to accommodate a coffin and pallbearers.

I put my arm around James and tried to comfort him. "Sweetheart, sometimes when certain conditions are just right, people can see a picture of the past playing out right in front of them. No one really knows how or why it happens, but it does," I explained. "Sometimes people like us see it more often, because it takes a kind of openness to it that my family's always had. That includes you now too." James nodded.

"Sometimes, in a really emotional situation like that, an imprint is made. But it's nothing to be afraid of, it can't hurt you in any way, it's just kinda weird." I smiled down at him, heart full and bursting with love. I smoothed his hair back from his forehead and kissed it, breathing in his smell, then hugged him for good measure.

"Mommy loves you and will never let anything hurt you," I told him.

That seemed to calm him. He hopped down and, with a quick grin, ran off to play, tossing back a quick air kiss, and a "Love you, Mom." Slowly, James learned about these strange paranormal things, and it kept him from being frightened.

Not long after that, I was up late one night, reading, when I felt something. I looked up from my book, and standing next to the fireplace in the adjacent room was a tall young man with shoulder-length dark hair and a beard. He looked to be in his late twenties and was wearing a red plaid shirt and dark suspenders. He stood with his arms calmly at his sides, watching me. His body blocked my view of the fireplace, so he seemed as solid as you or me. I felt icy cold as the unreality of it hit me.

The hair on my arms stood up. I gave a little shriek and looked away quickly, shocked, thinking I wasn't seeing what I was seeing! When I looked back, he was gone. He didn't feel threatening in any way. He'd just calmly been watching what I was doing.

I've never seen him again.

Another common sight in our house is a whitish mist that forms on the landing at the top of the stairs. Many times James commented on it; we'd watch it form, then dissipate. Others sometimes saw it too and asked about it. James never wanted to scare his friends, so he'd always say he wasn't sure. Then, if I was within hearing distance, he'd smile at me, our little secret secure.

A fellow psychic once told me that she saw a spirit named Charles around me. After finding the abstract on the house, I discovered that the original owner's son was named Charles, and he was the last owner of the house in the seventies. I believe it's Charles who stays here with us, and Charles who James saw as a baby, and who I saw as a young man. As long as he stays in the attic, I can deal with it!

————

It's always helped me to hear about others who've had haunted experiences, I guess because it made me feel less alone. It's amazing how many do believe; one-third of Americans believe in ghosts and almost one-half believe in psychic abilities. Then again, there may be those who don't even recognize they *have* a ghost.

We were invited to the wedding of an old friend. Afterwards, we went back to the little house they'd just bought. Along with friends and family, we watched them open their presents. I was handed the gift book register and asked to enter the gifts. The gift book set included a fancy long feather pen.

Pen poised to paper, I waited for the first name and entered it. Suddenly, while waiting for the next gift, the pen was almost pulled away from me by the feather at the end of it! *What the heck is going on here?* I thought, *That was really weird.* I inspected the pen; it looked normal; just a big silly pen with a footlong feather curling from the end! I placed the tip back on the page and it was pushed this time, as though by unseen fingers grabbing it above mine. *Dear God, something's trying to take over the pen,* my brain screamed. My senses started to tingle and I suddenly knew I wasn't alone.

I stopped listening to the gifts announced and struggled to hold the pen upright as it was pushed and pulled, apparently trying to make me write something! Like some diabolical slapstick skit, we wrestled for control of the pen. I jerked it away entirely and held it down at my side for a moment, gathering my composure, as embarrassed by this threat to my "normal" façade as I was frightened by the nature of it.

"What was that name again?" I shakily asked my friend's new wife. She repeated it and began to open a new present.

"Oh how nice, a toaster, and we really need one," she announced happily in her "member of the normal world" status.

Please stop it, I silently begged whoever was grabbing the pen. Then reluctantly, I put it back up to the page again, trying to catch up with the gifts. A sickening feeling of unreality descended upon me in the midst of this all-too-normal domestic scene. I was alone with this "thing." Normal people in the room went about the normal business of oohing and ahhing over the gifts. Once again, the disparity between normal and me reared its ugly head. *Maybe I'm just imagining it,* I thought. But once again there was the pressure on the pen, pushed and pulled by an insistent, unseen hand. *STOP IT!* I wanted to scream, but instead, as calmly as possible, I asked if someone else could please enter the gifts, as my hand was hurting. The lady who offered didn't seem to have any problems with the pen.

I sat frozen and watchful for the next hour, all senses on high alert, testing the atmosphere, feeling for negative energy and danger. But though I could feel some presence, it didn't feel malevolent. I wondered if it was the home's former owner, an old lady who'd died there years before, according to my friend. I feel bad now that I didn't let it happen, but wow, how could I have explained messages from the spirit world written all over their pretty little gift book? It scared me, coming at such an unexpected time and place. They don't always follow *our* rules of etiquette, that's for sure.

———

I'd been doing readings for friends, and letting clairvoyance happen naturally—not really understanding that I could call it up on demand. At first the feelings had come when I least expected them, and they didn't always seem useful—wouldn't it be better not to know about danger than to be constantly reminded there might be some lurking about? Eventually I saw the practical applications possible. James was still young when I tried to use it to help *myself*…only to learn it doesn't often work that way.

I'd taken a job of holding teen dances at a park on summer weekends. It was popular and very busy. For my birthday, I'd received a beautiful necklace, a blue topaz set in gold, encircled with diamonds. I loved it and wore it that night.

After the dance, we went about our cleanup. I realized the snap-on hinge on my necklace had come loose sometime during the evening. The beautiful topaz necklace fob was gone. Just the gold chain was around my neck.

The area was huge and mostly grass. I was inconsolable, knowing the necklace was probably gone forever. We looked everywhere on the routes I walked, but found nothing. James even helped look too, with all the energy of youth. Since it was dark, my assistant manager and I decided to come back the next day to search with a metal detector.

I could barely sleep that night, I was so worried about the necklace. We arrived early the next day and began. It was truly a daunting task, just so much acreage to cover, and I began to accept that it was hopeless. But suddenly I thought of the psychic ability and decided to try it. I sat down and covered my eyes, waiting to see what would happen. The "light" began to form a picture; a perfectly shaped pair of red lips. Suddenly the lips spit out the topaz fob!

This was so clear and startling, and accompanied by a sense of knowing, that I shouted to my assistant manager, "Hey, I think it's around the drinking fountain!" Since I'd seen the lips spit out the necklace, I connected lips with either drinking or spitting water. So we headed to the fountain and searched all around. Nothing. Then I thought, *well, maybe it meant the restroom sinks, since there's running water there to drink from.*

We searched high and low, but no necklace. I'd given up, it was hopeless and the necklace was gone forever. We walked dejectedly back toward our cars.

"I want to look one more time at the fountain. You go on ahead," I said. I felt so sure when I had the vision. I got on my hands and knees, feeling around the grass at the concrete base, when I heard my assistant manager shout from a football field length away: "Hey, I found it!" I ran to him. And when I heard his story, the gift in all its strangeness, got even stranger.

My assistant manager was a Skoal user. Anyone who knows, knows this form of tobacco use involves a lot of spitting of juice. "I was walking down the path toward the cars," he said, "when I looked down to spit, and saw something shining in the grass."

My mouth was hanging open in amazement. I'd been interpreting the picture of lips spitting out the necklace as where we'd *find* it; at a place where lips would be, like a drinking fountain. But it was showing me *how* it'd be found, by my assistant manager almost spitting on it! This was clairvoyance, precognition, and premonition all wrapped into one. This is the first time I understood how difficult it'd be to interpret what I'm seeing at any given time.

This also showed me that clairvoyance could be used more effectively. I set about refining it in order to be more useful. And I experimented a lot.

8

Nightmares and Nuance

I was riding in the back seat of a car. Suddenly there was an incredibly violent, wrenching movement, and the screeching, grinding, and high-pitched shrieking of tearing metal.

I felt myself rising up out of my body, straight up through the roof, and I knew I'd died. As I ascended, I saw I was in a concrete tunnel with lights along the upper walls. Up, up, I rose, until I finally came to the Gates of Heaven, where a crowd had gathered. I felt nothing but peace after the terrible experience moments before. It was now calm, serene, and beautiful. People walked toward me with their arms outstretched to greet me. They were so happy to see me, but I didn't seem to know them.

I was amazed at this reception by strangers, but began warming toward them all as I continued slowly through the throng. As they were touching my hands, and saying how glad they were to see me, I heard James's voice.

"Mom, wake up!" he said, wanting his breakfast made.

I jumped and woke from the most realistic dream I'd ever had. "Honey, I was having the craziest dream," I told him.

I can't tell him I know I'm going to die in a terrible car wreck soon, I thought, *probably on our trip to Florida.* We'd been counting down the days until we headed to Walt Disney World for our annual vacation. We drove down, and the tunnels through the mountains looked just like the one I saw in the dream. I even got into the back seat at times to take a nap while Rod drove. *Maybe if I don't do that on this trip, I'll be okay*, I thought. I knew beyond a shadow of a doubt that I was going to die in this wreck. I could feel it in every fiber of my being. I wasn't very scared though, mainly because I knew that I was going to Heaven. That sense of "knowing" was a feeling I can't describe, except to say I knew for certain. It made me scared to die that way, but also reassured me of my destination. But I *was* worried about the wreck itself; about my family, who'd be in the car with me.

I told Rod, and eventually told James, and would've canceled the trip, if not for the following week's events. We were watching TV when the bulletins came on. Diana, Princess of Wales, had been killed in a car wreck

in France. She'd been in the back seat with her boyfriend when their driver smashed into a concrete col-
umn in a tunnel while trying to outrun paparazzi.

"Look, Mom," James said, pointing to the TV as I
sat in shock, "there's the tunnel you described. Is that it?"

They showed pictures of the car and the tunnel I'd seen
in my dream, the same lights on the sides. I knew then that
for some reason, I was shown her death, and I was "her" for
that moment when she died and rose to Heaven.

"Yes, honey, that's it," I told him, amazed.

The only explanation I have is that I'd always been
interested in the Royal Family, and followed Diana's life
and read her books. But I've never understood why I
experienced this. It's not as though I was shown that it
would happen to Diana. It had happened to me.

So I guess I wasn't meant to interfere and try to stop it.
That, too, would have been impossible; it was very doubtful
she'd listen even if I *could* get through to her. I was simply
supposed to know her destination was Heaven. Maybe
this was meant to comfort me. It's of no practical use in a
case like this, except maybe to strengthen or enlighten me
personally. I'll never understand, at least not while I'm still
a part of this world.

———

I'd always had qualms about charging for readings and
only took tips, but it eventually became necessary, to help
pay the bills. The whole idea of these or any "gifts" being

used to make money worried me. Then again, I've always felt guilty for making money with musical gifts too, having been taught God's gifts should be used for God. But if someone is good at something they do, it could be said it's their gift, and we all need to eat. Friends would ask for readings, then friends of friends; it spread by word of mouth. I'd oblige, then get scared when eerily accurate information would come through for them.

Finally, when people asked for readings, I started taking appointments and charging. Voila! Suddenly I was a professional psychic.

———

Learning to interpret, or how *not* to interpret the information given clairvoyantly has been my most difficult problem. Once there was a girl at a reading party whose advance reading made me pause—simply because it seemed so silly. Behind my closed eyes, I'd seen the light clearly form a picture of a round stylist's hairbrush! *Maybe she's a hairdresser or something*, I thought. Aware that I was judging and interpreting and shouldn't be, I wrote it down in case it meant something to her.

When she sat for her reading at the party, I gave her several names I'd received clairvoyantly—one of which was her boss who had just fired her. And finally, even though I was afraid of looking foolish, I mentioned the hairbrush. She smiled and shook her head.

"While I was driving over here today," she began, "I felt something bumping up against my heel every time I stopped." She laughed and went on, "I reached down while I was at the light and felt around for it, picked it up, and saw it was my mom's round stylist's hairbrush."

Now why in the world had her clairvoyant reading ten days before the party shown me this very brush? I think it was just for validation—on both our parts. Sometimes I think it's just a sign that I'm seeing something authentic, which helps me have the confidence to continue on just as much as it helps the hearer to be open and believe.

I remember two younger girls I read for who were part of a group of girls. They were best friends. As I gave each one a private reading, I heard the name of a woman, spoken very insistently.

"There's a Grandma Hazel coming through," I told the first girl. She looked quite puzzled and said she didn't know anyone by that name. So I chalked it up to a bad connection and moved on. During the next reading for her friend, another insistent voice came through.

"There seems to be a Grandma Beth coming through for you." As I relayed this, I was met with another puzzled look. Now I was getting embarrassed by my lack of accuracy! But I explained how sometimes others jump in, and maybe it was information meant for someone else in her group. As I finished my final reading that evening and was packing up my bag, the two friends burst into the room.

"Remember Grandma Hazel who came through for me, and the Grandma Beth you told her about?" asked the first girl.

"Yes I do," I said, wondering what this was about, since neither name had meant anything to them.

"Well, you had them mixed up. *My* Grandma was Beth, and *hers* was Hazel!" She laughed excitedly, pointing at her friend. "We sat together on the patio comparing notes and realized what had happened. Both our grandmas came through to say hi to us, but just got their timing a little mixed up!"

I explained how sometimes even random information comes in for somebody's close friend or relative, which I like to call "jumping on." When one spirit's message gets through, I believe it creates excitement for others around them and they all start to impart information. It can really be confusing. It's like a giant batch of puzzle pieces, and each one goes somewhere. For a psychic, sometimes finding exactly where is the hardest thing.

———

James grew older and I got the R. A. under control. One day, an old friend called me about forming a local rock band. *That might be fun*, I thought. Even though I'd taken a nine-year hiatus from performing while raising James, suddenly I was back. It was local version of what I'd been doing on a national level. I loved it!

I'd been writing songs the whole time that I'd been a full-time mom, and recording them in my home studio. I decided to send them to publishers. I got some interest and offers to sign song contracts and finally realized that I could focus on being a songwriter while still being a mom and living a good life off the road. My old obsession/ambition shifted to this new goal, kicked in full force, and I was off—once again striving to be "the best" at something and hating myself whenever I wasn't.

I made trips to Nashville to meet with publishers interested in signing me, and on one trip, I brought James and his friend. We were all sitting in my new publisher's office, which also had a recording studio attached next door. It wasn't a formal meeting; I'd signed the contracts the day before and had just stopped in to say goodbye, planning on a day of sightseeing before heading home.

On his best behavior, James sat smiling politely at the publisher as we made small talk.

"Thanks for the great tips on where to take the kids," I said. "We're heading to the Hermitage as soon as we leave."

"I'm glad to help," my new publisher drawled. "Hope you enjoy yourselves."

I couldn't help but notice white clouds of smoke had begun to pour through the air vent near the ceiling. I didn't want to say anything, but maybe there was a fire!

"Umm, there seems to be some smoke coming in from somewhere," I finally said, pointing at the vent. I wasn't getting any psychic warning vibes, so I wasn't sure what was happening! Just then, the smell from the smoke hit me. It was pot!

"Oh, that must be coming from the studio next door," the publisher said, chuckling. I laughed as well, and James picked that moment to ask if they could use the restroom, which happened to be accessed by the shared hallway to the studio.

"Sure," answered the publisher.

"Behave yourselves," I sternly told thirteen-year-old James and his friend as they rushed out to try to see the excitement in the next room. I doubted they actually needed to use the bathroom.

We were saying our goodbyes when James and friend burst back in, in high excitement.

"Mom, Mom," he stage-whispered, tugging my arm. He knew not to do anything rude while I was conducting business, so this must be important!

"What's going on over there?" I laughed.

"Mom, it's Ludacris!"

"What's ludicrous?" I answered, flabbergasted he'd act up in front of a stranger.

"No, Mom, it's Ludacris, the rapper, right there in the hallway, we said hi to each other!" he blurted.

Well, I wouldn't have known Ludacris from Ridiculous, and didn't know that he was a huge up-and-coming star in the rap world. But the kids sure did, and they talked about it for months afterwards. So my songwriting, previously pretty much ignored by James at that age as "uncool," took on a whole new cachet after that!

———

Time passed and James grew up fast. He had several obsessions going on at any given moment, which was typical. Music, aggressive skating, and skateboarding were the top three jockeying for position as he moved into his teens. He was a natural at music, and when he entered a couple of local talent contests, winning money for first place, that hooked him. Whatever consumed him at that very moment was all he could see, and there was no room for anything else—it was all or nothing. He'd inherited my sometimes obsessive and ambitious ways, wanting to achieve and do his best in his areas of interest. Though I'd hoped he wasn't cursed with my perfectionism, he seemed to adopt it anyway.

He saw an ad on one of the skateboard sites for a new company in L.A. They were looking for skateboarders from the Midwest for a pro team, focusing on giving younger kids the chance to be sponsored. They already had their California team. James was obsessed with being chosen. He practiced every spare minute—in blowing snow, dark of night, it didn't matter. He spent hours every day with our video camera, filming "sections" of his best tricks for the audition tape.

Finally James's tape was finished. In the intro, he gave a heartfelt speech about how badly he wanted to join the team and how willing he was to promote the company as a Midwest team rider. I helped him package it and send it off.

About a week later, the phone rang, and it was for James. I lurked around trying to hear the conversation. The owner told James that at age fifteen, he was older than they'd been accepting, but they'd made an exception due to his skills and how badly he wanted to join the team.

"Mom, Mom, I've been accepted!" James yelled, hanging up. I was almost as happy as he was.

Over the next couple weeks, the company sent skateboards, which James used and displayed, generating orders for the company. We had promo shots taken of him holding their skateboard. He spent lots of time on the phone with the owner discussing the company and boarding in general. James lobbied for a friend to be sponsored, and he was.

Then James started pushing to go to California; the owner wanted the Midwest team to come out. I had no rest. James was relentless.

"James, stop!" I told him. "If all goes well, maybe I'll drive you out next summer."

"Mom, that's not soon enough," he whined. "He wants the Midwest riders to come out now for a week and meet the West Coast team."

"James, I can't do it now. I know you're excited, but we don't even know this guy. He could be anyone."

"Mom, you're so paranoid! I'll let you talk to him next time, you'll see, he's fine. I never get to do ANY-THING other kids get to do! This is my big break and you're ruining it!" James knew this wasn't at all true, but it sounded good at the moment. Plus he knew how weak I was where he was concerned.

"Aww honey," I said. "Let me think about it. Maybe we can work something out."

James jumped up and hugged me, excited. He knew how to get around me, and that this meant I'd probably relent.

I felt bad and thought maybe I could let him go alone as the owner had suggested; James's friend who'd gotten sponsored said he'd be allowed to go, so maybe I could put them both on a plane and they'd be just fine. After all, James was almost sixteen. But he was a very young look-ing fifteen, small in stature, thin from constant skating and skateboarding. He looked more like a twelve-year-old.

The next night James came running, cordless phone in hand, saying the owner wanted to talk to me.

"Hello," I said, "I'm glad I finally get to 'meet' you! James is so excited to be signed to your company!"

"Hello ma'am, I'm glad to finally get to talk to you, too. James told me you had some reservations about him com-ing here, and I wanted to reassure you I'd take care of him like my own," he answered.

The moment I heard his voice, I got a terrible feeling, and heard "NO" loudly in my head—it almost reverberated. I was so startled, I paused for a moment, not wanting to give myself away.

"Yes, I was thinking of ways that we could send him soon," I lied. "I originally intended to bring him out myself next summer, but maybe we can work it out sooner." The man talked on for a few more minutes, friendly as could be, but I *knew*, absolutely and without a doubt, something was terribly wrong, and no way was James going out there. The hard part was going to be breaking the news to James. I didn't really have the nerve, and hoped I could put him off for a while.

That night I did a search of who to contact in L.A. to do a background check of a business, and came up with the county sheriff's department. I sent an email inquiring about this man and his company. Early the next morning, I called the department.

"I'm happy to say the man has no record of any kind," the deputy said. "But I've got to tell you, I'm impressed that you cared enough to call. Most parents don't."

"He's my only child, and I'm a little obsessive about him," I laughed. Something still didn't feel right, I knew by now to mostly pay attention to the "little voice" and I'd already decided I wasn't sending James, clean record or not.

When James got home from school and I told him I'd called the L.A. Sheriff's Department, he thought it was really funny and teased me for a while.

"Way to go, Mom, always looking for a pervert!" he laughed. I laughed too, but inside I knew he wasn't going and it wasn't funny!

That night, after he'd spent some time on the phone with the owner, he ran down to tell me what happened.

"Mom, I told him you called the sheriff on him and did a background check." He laughed. "He was really upset! He kept saying, 'Why would she *run* me like that? Why did she think something was wrong?' I told him that's just the way you are,"—he snickered—"and I'm used to it!"

Over the next couple weeks, James pestered me relentlessly. I told him we just didn't have the money. He forlornly told me the Midwest team had gone out, including a kid he'd made friends with in Pennsylvania. Meanwhile, James got distracted and didn't talk to the owner for a couple weeks. One night he yelled from the attic for me to come up. I did reluctantly, as I still didn't like it up there.

"Mom, you're not going to believe this," James said, shocked. "Look." He pointed at the computer screen, which had a story about the skateboard company owner. There'd been complaints from around the country and the Feds did a raid, finding dozens of videotapes of underage kids, drunk or drugged, with him performing sex acts on them. He was a known pedophile, recently released from prison, but he'd changed his name and didn't report as a sex offender—that's why he didn't show up on the cop's radar. That's also why he was after younger kids for his skate team. The poor kid from Pennsylvania was one of those on the tapes. I thanked God and the "little voice" for saving James. And James, cowed now and uncharacteristically quiet, hugged me and said he was sorry for yelling at me about it. I must admit, I used this ammo shamelessly for many years, every time he needed reminded that sometimes Mom *did* know best.

————

James was soon old enough to drive, and I bought him a reliable car to run around town and get to work.

As he became an adult, he tried on personas as other people tried on clothes, becoming fascinated with characters as wildly diverse as Jack Kerouac and Hunter S. Thompson and Jack White. He didn't adopt their personalities, but was always adding bits and pieces of them to himself, on the road to finding out who he was. He held many jobs, never liking any of them for too long, which led to a lot of talks from me.

We encouraged him to do the things that made him happiest, that he was good at, but I still worried about him. Floating through life was his style, and I was an attentive mother for longer than most—because of his ADD, his only-child status, and my love for him. My illness had taught me that life is potentially short and very precious. I honestly didn't think I'd live very long and I wanted to lavish as much love and attention on him as I could in case I wasn't there when he grew up.

We grew very close, and he felt able to talk to me about almost anything.

"Mom, I'm giving up skateboarding completely and focusing on aggressive rollerblading," James told me one day. After his bad skateboarding experience, he started traveling to aggressive skating competitions all over the country with older friends. I was so nervous the first couple times I let him go, but I trusted his friends to look after him. I couldn't justify keeping him home. He got his first picture/interview profile in *Daily Bread* magazine, the skaters "bible" of the time, and was on cloud nine. His dreams were all coming true, and more than anything, I wanted to support his dreams because mine had been stopped cold by my illness.

———

One of James's best friends, a fellow aggressive skater from Detroit, came to stay for the weekend. By then, James had made his bedroom up in the attic, with no seeming ill effects. They'd stay up half the night playing music, talking with friends on instant messenger, and plotting which skate spots they'd hit the next day.

It was getting late, and Gary decided he wanted a midnight snack. We considered all James's friends part of the family, so Gary headed down to the kitchen for a sandwich. As he stood at the counter, he heard the sound of the basement door being pushed open. Our pets were Sara the German shepherd and a cat called Mr. Cat. Our basement door was always kept on a chain lock so that the dog couldn't eat the cat food just inside the door on the landing.

Mr. Cat had a habit of coming up from the basement and pushing the door open until it was stopped by the chain, a few inches' gap, just enough for Mr. Cat to go in or out, but not enough to let Sara the cat-food-loving German shepherd in. The door chain made a distinctive rattle each time he came and went.

Gary had heard Mr. Cat come and go a hundred times, so he knew this noise. He headed toward the basement door, calling "Here Kitty, Kitty," but no Mr. Cat. Then he remembered Mr. Cat was in the attic! Maybe he was hearing things, he thought. He got his plate, shut off the light, and headed up the servants' staircase. About two or three steps up, he literally froze.

"Something just went through me!" he yelled. He ran up the stairs toward the attic and met James coming down in response to his yell.

"You know how you've always said you have a ghost? I think I just met it!"

"Yeah, it's pretty cool," said James nonchalantly. "It's nothing to be afraid of."

Since it didn't seem like a big deal to James, Gary slept easy that night. Could it have followed him down from the attic, wondering who this was, making sure he wasn't up to something in "its" house?

Our rock band eventually fizzled out and I began to play in acoustic duos, eventually doing solo gigs as well. I was busy, playing several nights per week, most weeks of the year. Obsessed with it all once again, I couldn't seem to turn down any job offers. I took steroids and strong meds to be able to play so often, but even so, my fingers began to get the classic R.A. deformities. I adapted my playing accordingly. Music still kept me sane and focused, and I counted on the income, too. I released my first CD, and it sold well. I also continued doing readings, at least, when I had time! My second CD also did well, which led to more trips and publishing contracts.

Walking into the courtyard of a restaurant where I was performing one evening, I passed by one of my reading clients, and she called me over to her table. I'd always tried to balance my music career with readings in order to fulfill as many requests as I could, but sometimes it was hard. During tourist season, I'm booked solid with gigs. This lady had been waiting a while and I felt bad. She introduced her three friends, two ladies and a younger man, and began telling them about my readings—how I'd helped her and how accurate they were. I could see their skepticism as I politely smiled and thanked her. She was a nice woman and I liked her.

"Show them how you do it," she gushed. I felt embarrassed, as I usually do in these situations. It's not something you can always call forth on demand, and I was in "music mode." The more nervous or stressed I am, the less likely I'll be open enough to hear or see anything. Plus in public, I don't want to close my eyes to see what pictures form. It's embarrassing enough without that! I usually just listen for what I'm told clairaudiently or clairvoyantly, which isn't always as reliable when crowd noise or information is interfering. I also try to "turn off" as much as possible when I'm in music mode or it gets too overwhelming. Unfortunately, any psychic clients in the audience don't know this.

"Well, I don't know, I'm not really on the psychic clock tonight," I laughed, disconcerted.

She pointed to her girlfriend beside her. "What do you see for her?" she asked point blank.

Okay, here goes, I thought, unable to avoid it. I looked at the woman's face and the name McCallister popped into my head. "I'm not getting much," I said, "but the name McCallister comes to me for some reason. Is that a name you know?" Suddenly the woman had a serious, almost worried look on her face.

"That's the name of the street I live on," she replied. "Is something going to happen?" The lady I knew squealed and clapped her hands while the other woman asked, "How did you know that?"

"I honestly don't know," I replied, feeling somewhat like a circus act. "It just happens sometimes. It doesn't mean something's going to happen either. Sometimes it's just a validation that it's working."

At this point the young man at the table was staring intently at me. "What can you tell me about myself," he asked. "Can you tell me what my calling is?'

As I glanced at him, I saw a picture of knives chopping vegetables, and the word "chef" was spoken in my head.

"You should be a chef," I told him. "You'd be very happy."

"I've always wanted to be a chef!" he blurted. "But I didn't think I could do it. I even looked into culinary school when I was younger. How did you know?"

"I don't know how, I just do," I told him. "You should take this seriously, and yes you *can* do it!"

Feeling somewhat shy at what now seemed like showing off, I explained that I'd always believed it was a gift from God meant to help people, and when it was working, it was amazing.

They both thanked me, and then I told them I had to get ready to play. I promised my client I'd do her reading soon.

"What about me?" asked the other woman at the table. "Do you see anything?"

My playing partner was on the stage looking at his watch, and I was torn between these people and the job I was hired for that night.

"Umm, I'm not getting much," I said, glancing from her to the stage, distracted and needing to get up there.

Suddenly a picture of an arrowhead flashed in my mind, and I decided to trust it, because it's all I had!

"I'm seeing an arrowhead for some reason," I told her. She looked awed and said, "I live on Arrowhead Lane."

"It must be a night for addresses!" I laughed, turning toward the stage. My friend excitedly thanked me, and I saw her companions watching me curiously the rest of the night, weighing the evidence they'd received.

I've found that very often, this ability scares people, just like it scared me. Even those who claim to want to know don't know what to make of it. They expect "you will meet a tall dark handsome stranger," not something specific. For those who get something specific, I try to use humor to soften the scariness. Because let's face it, some things you just don't want to know. And when some normal-looking, middle-aged woman pulls this stuff out of thin air, it's shocking. I do understand this completely.

Later at home, about four o'clock the next morning, there was a huge crash; the house literally shook. We bolted out of bed and looked out front—there was James's nice little Ford Escort wagon, rear end pushed up to the center of the car, totaled.

"Mom, my car is destroyed!" James cried. A trail of radiator fluid led away into the distance, and a license plate lay amongst the debris. Our neighbor had seen a van disentangle itself and drive away. The cops had only to follow the radiator fluid, and call in the plate number, and the drunk driver was arrested. Luckily, insurance paid for James's next car. This time the "darkness" didn't win, so it tried harder.

9

The Nature of the Beast

I continued to dance around my psychic abilities, focusing equally on music—completely absorbed by whatever I was doing at any moment. Staying stressed was also the best way I knew to deal with stress, since I wouldn't have time to think about it! Even though I tried to keep music and psychic stuff separate, many times it presented itself through music connections.

A young woman named Sarah, who waitressed at a restaurant I played, asked me to read her palm and I saw she was pregnant before she knew it, and that it was a boy. She became a believer and planned a "psychic party," where I'm hired for private readings at someone's house and do reading for their friends.

I always ask for the first names of all those attending so I can do more extensive clairvoyant readings for each name in advance. I close my eyes, ask how to help them, and behind my closed eyelids, the light forms pictures, words, or symbols. It sounds crazy, but it's true.

At their reading, I do a tarot layout, read their palms, and relay any names or images sent to me clairvoyantly, which sometimes happens while touching their hands.

Sarah gave me the party list; all female names except for the last one, Evan. Prior to the party, I did my usual reading for each of the girls, writing down what was shown to me. Then finally I came to Evan.

Please show me how to help this boy, and what he needs to know, I prayed. Then I waited and watched as the light formed—testicles. Yes. Okay. I stopped and tried again. Same thing. I could see inside them, the dense round shape glistening as it slowly turned, showing every millimeter of the shiny smooth surface. *But wait—what was that*—suddenly I'd noticed on one of the testicles what looked like a lump. Was I seeing this because he was the only male on the list? *No way am I going to say anything and risk being wrong,* I thought. *How embarrassing!*

Always, there was my chronic self-doubt. Well aware that imagination sometimes wants to fill in the gaps, sometimes it takes all my courage to tell what I see. But by this time I'd learned it was best to relay the pictures without too much interpretation. Psychic information is like a puzzle, and the pieces need to be carefully assembled to get the whole picture. And the pieces are best assembled by the person being read. I'd now had enough experience to know these odd messages turn out to be some of the most special for the receiver. So I wouldn't edit myself simply for my ego's sake. If I was wrong and looked like a fool, so be it.

The day of the party, I met Sarah outside the restaurant. As I pulled up, she jumped out of her car and waved. "Hey there!" she called. "Good to see you again. All the girls are so excited!" We hugged and I decided to ask the embarrassing question as delicately as I could.

"Sarah, I've got a crazy question," I began, "and I don't quite know how to tactfully put this."

"You should know by now you can ask me anything," she answered sweetly. "What is it?"

"Well, can you tell me who Evan is?"

"He's my fiancé!" She laughed, a big smile lighting up her young face. "We live together!"

Okay, great, I thought. *This may be a bit easier than I assumed. Here goes.* "Well, I know this is strange, but can you tell me, has he ever had any problem with his testicles?" I truly thought I was about to be humiliated since these were people in their early twenties with all their parts still in working order!

An incredulous look came over Sarah's face. "He's had a lump for a long time. He's been to several doctors and they all tell him nothing's wrong."

So it was for real then, and *very* accurate. *Whew, what a relief!* I told her it was being shown to me because it was important, and he needed to follow up on it. I also asked her if she'd take Evan aside and tell him, in case he'd rather not discuss it with a total stranger. In truth, *I* was hoping not to have to discuss it!

"No problem, I'll tell him," she said.

Turns out I was the only one worried. Evan brought it up himself when he came in for his reading. "Yeah, I've been checking on it," he told me. "But it's really bizarre you could see it."

No matter how many times this happens, I am always totally amazed and humbled. I believe only God could know these things. But still, I asked myself: *Why me?*

———

James got sponsored by several skate and clothing companies and spent all his time practicing or conducting business online. He ate, slept, and breathed aggressive skating. On warm summer nights, and well into fall and winter, I'd hear him across the street at the Laundromat practicing: the clang of skates sliding on rails, the clack of hard landings on concrete, the laughter of the friends who always surrounded him. These sounds are omnipresent in any memory of James, woven into his comings and goings to Atlanta, Pittsburgh, Detroit, L.A. This was quintessential James, moving fast, on wheels, always headlong into the next adventure.

His best friend the last couple years of high school was a quiet boy who was a bit younger. He'd had a rough family life dealing with divorces and chaos, and his mother was a heavy drinker. He loved skating almost as much as James, and it cemented their friendship. James often picked out the broken ones in life; it seemed to be his path.

When one of the boys' mutual friends committed suicide, they were devastated. It was their first taste of death. James and I went to calling hours with his friend and his mother. Not long after that, I went to a club downtown to see James's band play, and the mother was there, very drunk, barely able to stand. I thanked God for my path. No amount of freedom or partying even came close to the joy I'd had in being James's mom. I tried to give her son attention and acceptance. He was a nice boy and eventually James and he drifted apart.

———

Life went on and, through word of mouth, I did more readings. I was surprised by how the work came because I really didn't advertise much and wanted to remain low-key, still fighting my religious upbringing about whether or not I should even be *doing* psychic work. I sometimes heard the old witch's voice in my head and thought about the "darkness." Yet the times when I helped someone, it felt like my calling and like it was from God.

I met author and paranormal investigator Sherri Brake of Haunted Heartland Tours at a ghost hunt and dinner she held at the old Zoar Hotel—the place I'd played in its glory days when I was a teenager. I'd heard about the event online and corresponded with Sherri via email.

Eager to meet Sherri, I'd brought her an old photo of the hotel. I held it in my hand as I descended the hill overlooking Zoar. At first sight, the brooding old hotel, long abandoned, looked almost the same as it had thirty years before. But on closer inspection, I saw the peeling paint and shutters hanging askance. The memories rushed back: this was where my abuser came to hear me when I was just nineteen. *I've lived three lifetimes since then, no thanks to him,* I thought.

After Sherri and I talked, we set a lunch date, where I did an impromptu palm reading. After clairvoyantly "seeing," among other things, a seashell (she was going to the ocean on a long-planned family trip) and a Mercedes emblem (her husband worked at a Mercedes dealership), she asked if I'd like to do readings occasionally for her company. We've been friends ever since.

I met Laura Lyn, who also reads sometimes for Sherri's events, when I went for one of the quick readings she offered.

"Hi, I'm Debra," I said. "I'm a palm reader and psychic as well," I told Laura. "I'm going to be doing readings for Sherri also." And suddenly a name was spoken in my mind. I told Laura the name and asked who he was.

Unfortunately, she said, it was her ex and she'd just come through a difficult divorce. I apologized and explained the name was given so strongly, I knew she must've been through a rough time.

The next time we met, we were on a tour bus going to a haunted prison with Sherri. Again, I was given a name for her, spoken insistently, so I knew it was important. "He's the new relationship in my life," she laughed.

I was glad to tell her it looked like they were going to be happy, at least for the near future. Though they did eventually go their separate ways, luckily, after that strange first and second impression, I can still count Laura as a friend. What happened was an example of clairaudience at its best—it can be quite helpful sometimes. But it can also be confusing. It was wonderful to be able to tell Laura her relationship would be good for a while. But with other relationships in my own life, information wasn't always forthcoming.

———

After over fifty years together, my parents were still in love. They were just as playful as ever with each other. Mom was the rock who held the family together, a traditional housewife in every sense. And Mom doted on James, her little baby. Then Mom got sick; it was a rare brain tumor. After surgery and radiation, the doctor took us aside.

"She might lose some memory and have some blurred vision," he told us, "but we won't know exactly how this will affect things until about eight months from now."

Nearly eight months to the day later, Mom went completely blind. It was devastating. Then, the radiation began to give her dementia. Though the doctors were shocked at her poor outcome, her new mental state was a blessing in disguise. She became very accepting and childlike. Dad and I shouldered all the caretaking associated with the change in her, but for the most part she was oblivious and even happy most of the time.

Eventually, she had to be moved to a nursing home. And six weeks later, she passed away. Dad was crushed, lost deep in grief, and I truly thought he'd be one of those widowers who pass away shortly after their mates of a broken heart, as Rod's dad had.

We visited him often, had him over, and nothing helped.

"Dad, promise me you'll go to the Senior Center on Monday," I pleaded. "Maybe you can eat lunch with your old friends and play cards or something." He agreed and began going. I relaxed a little, hoping time would ease his grief. He'd been such a devoted husband and loving father, he deserved peace in his golden years.

———

The insistent voices of clairaudience often broke through for someone else. It was always clear then, and I listened and reported. But in my own life, I didn't always listen. I never quite knew if my everyday feelings of danger were random neuroticism or something important. I still didn't want to admit how often my feelings were right. So I either overreacted, or didn't react at all. And when the fears concerned James, as they often did, he'd get mad if I brought them up, saying I was going to "jinx" him by saying them aloud. So I kept quiet unless it was too intense. It made him happier and me miserable.

James was in and out of the house for a couple years, and we enjoyed him while he was here. He moved in with a friend, but lost his job and moved back home again. He insulated our old garage, dreaming of starting a skate shop there, and used it for a hangout in the meantime.

He'd have friends over to his "shed," as they called it, and they'd stay up half the night, falling asleep on the floor or in the chairs scattered throughout the garage. James had a bed and dresser out there, and a computer, and desk. He painted the famous "Welcome to Las Vegas" sign on the wall, and his decorating was complete. The old garage held heat well since he'd insulated it, so just a space heater kept it warm in winter. I worried incessantly about that heater because I kept having bad feelings. This was one of the times I couldn't keep quiet about it.

"James," I called, sticking my head into the garage, "I bought you a smoke alarm."

"Oh, Mom," James sighed, disgusted. "I knew you wouldn't stop until you got your way!"

James ridiculed me endlessly about it. I'd stop in to check it, only to find he'd taken the battery out to use in his guitar. 'Round and 'round we went.

Early one morning, I heard a lot of noise and woke to find James and his friends downstairs.

"James, what's going on?" I gasped, out of breath. He looked worried, unusual for James, and I knew right away it was serious.

"Mom, the smoke alarm woke us!" he said. "We were asleep and somehow one of the cushions got up against the heater and started a fire."

"Oh my God." I started for the back door, but James stopped me.

"No, it's okay, it's out now," he told me. "There's just a lot of smoke. But if the alarm hadn't gone off, it would've been way worse."

I ran to the garage to survey the damage: the fire had burned a hole in the rug and cushion—and had been starting up the wall, just inches from a sleeping friend.

"Oh James," I said, near tears. "I just knew something was gonna happen. Please, *please* be more careful. Don't ever take the battery out again. Come get one from me."

He and his friends stood solemnly watching, and finally he nodded.

"I promise, Mom. And by the way, thanks."

He now knew the smoke alarm thing wasn't just me being paranoid. But that didn't make me happy. I didn't want to be right; I wanted James to be safe. But the bad feelings continued, and I didn't know where they were coming from. I made James and any friends who stayed over sleep on the living room floor for a while.

Despite these occasional dramas, James entered young adulthood relatively unscathed. My son was in one piece. He was fine. I tried to relax, tried to ignore the feelings, tried hard to be "normal."

———

James Short grew into a dark-haired, green-eyed, handsome young man…who wanted to get tattoos in spite of the universal "Mom" warning: "Those tattoos are forever; you'll wish you didn't have them when you're old!" It didn't work. Since he'd been a child, he'd always said he'd die young (at twenty-five), and even though I told him we all felt that way at his age, he'd just shake his head. So the idea of tattoos on baggy skin didn't faze him.

"Mom, where are you?" he called to me from the front door one afternoon.

"In here, honey," I answered from the living room, putting my book down. He rounded the corner with a sheepish smile.

"Uh-oh," I said, "what's that look for? What are you up to now?"

"Well, I got something for you." Rolling up his sleeve, he displayed his forearm with a big red heart and a banner scrolling across it that read "MOM."

"Oh, James," I laughed.

"I was hoping it would make you like tattoos better," he said, smiling.

My heart melted. How could I be upset? I loved him so much! He always made me laugh, always defused any negative situation; he just had that playful way about him.

———

James soon became famous, even legendary, in the quirky world of extreme skating. The moves he invented and mastered, some daring, some technically precise, either made my blood run cold or left me in awe. His sense of balance in skating was matched only by his transparent love of life. James decided to drive Route 66 to California because it sounded cool. He got another tattoo: the lyrics from a favorite band about always being a child, never growing older. James was a free spirit, an old soul, yet eternally a child.

Not long after his West Coast trip, James decided he wanted to see New York City. He wanted to try being a busker in Times Square, playing guitar and singing for tips. So he did and loved it. It reinforced his feeling that he'd always be okay, no matter what.

———

My brother Dane, James's uncle, called me one day not long after the close call in the garage. Dane had moved away years before, but kept in touch. He'd grown up without much negativity in his life, and fulfilled his early promise and "mad scientist" ways by building an FM transmitter in our basement at age thirteen. He loved radio.

When he was old enough, he became a DJ, moving around the country, and finally settling into management. He's won a CMA for "Best Radio Station" and is a respected media executive. He's also accumulated a multimillion dollar vacation property business.

"Reb, you've got to watch it," he told me, after he sent me a video. "Check out the mirror in the master bedroom." Dane gave me my nickname at age twelve, and everyone still used it.

"Okay," I replied. "What is it?" But he wouldn't tell me.

It was a video of Dane touring a new condo, showing it to potential renters; he uploaded these onto his business website. I watched, smiling at his voice-over all through the downstairs. It brought back good memories of him playing DJ as a kid, narrating everything from home movies to ballgames. In the upstairs master bedroom, I got a cold chill and my heart skipped a beat as I saw what was reflected behind him in the mirror. I stopped the video and watched it frame by frame—there was a man there—*but the man in the mirror had no face.* You could see an ear, an eyebrow ridge, but where his features should be, it was blank. The eyebrow looked a little too slanted, a little too evil. I felt sick. Then I realized this man looked very familiar—the dark blond hair, the shape of his hairline, his head—could it be? He looked like the strange man with the otherworldly eyes who'd scared the crap out of me so many years ago at the nightclub! Impossible! But all my instincts told me it was him. I knew him, I recognized him, and he'd made quite an impression. But this time, he had no eyes. In dread, I called Dane immediately, and he explained what happened.

"Reb, I filmed this, got busy, and put it aside for a couple weeks," Dane said. "I finally remembered to watch and check it for mistakes before uploading it to the website."

He'd popped it in and watched the downstairs tour, on through to the upstairs master bedroom. After showcasing a TV/DVD player, the camera pans past the dresser mirror on his way out; and the "man" is seen reflected in the mirror, standing behind him in the hall—which he'd just walked through.

"When I saw it, I bolted out of my chair because I was there *alone!*" he told me.

"Dane, my God, are you *sure* some drifter didn't break in or follow you?"

"Absolutely not. The stairs and floor in the hall squeak, plus I'd just come through there, and went out the same way. No one was there! There's literally nowhere for them to go!" He was pretty shaken up. "Reb, look closely, the man has no face," he said worriedly. "There was no mirror behind me, and anyway, when I turn to leave, the 'man' stands still."

"I noticed that face thing," I told him, not wanting to mention that he looked like my "messenger." "I also noticed his feet look like they're moving, floating backwards to keep you from seeing him," I said. You could see the tracers of movement, the feet elongated, moving too fast to be caught on the frame by frame of the video. This truly frightened me. I tried to rationalize it, but couldn't, that terrible feeling again overpowering me. The "darkness" now had a face—well, not a face, but at least a form. But I'd seen his face all those years ago, and still remembered those eyes…

I decided I'd better tell Dane about the strange messenger in the club long ago.

I didn't expect him to have a similar story.

"Something happened to me right after I got to Chicago," Dane began. "I'd just got the radio station job doing the night shift, and didn't make much money. One really cold winter night, I stopped in the bank a block away to use the ATM, for a sandwich later at work. The bank was closed, but you could use your card to enter the foyer area where the ATM was."

"As I approached the door," Dane continued, "an old bag lady was huddled beside it. I held the door open and asked if she wanted to come in from the cold." Dane paused for a moment. "She thanked me and stepped inside," he said. "I put my card into the ATM, and punched in ten dollars, as I'd done lots of times at this same machine. I always got a crisp ten dollar bill. But for some reason, that night two fives came out."

"As I turned to leave," Dane continued, "I made a snap decision and handed her one of the fives, telling her to get some cocoa, since it was so cold. That's when she looked up at me, full in the face. Reb, her eyes were an unearthly light blue color." *Just like the guy in the club,* I thought.

"And then she spoke," Dane said. "May God bless you and give you more of that to spread around." *He sure did get a lot more of it!* I thought.

"It felt like it was set up, Reb," he went on, "like I was given the choice to be generous or to keep it for myself. Seriously, never before had two fives come from that machine—and I never had it happen again after that." *Was I also offered some choice somewhere, and did I mess it up?* I wondered. *I've always been pretty generous, but maybe it was something else that tested me.* My lifelong fears surfaced again. *Did I misuse my gifts?*

I thought about my life, all I'd gone through, and how Dane's life had been filled with light and positive outcomes. *I was the one who begged for the Ouija board. I was the one who invited something to come to me—and to be my friend!* Dane was just my unwitting partner. But I'd been just a kid who didn't know any better! And why would something be watching Dane? I was the one it focused on at Fifth Street. *Oh, that's just plain crazy*, I thought. *Maybe it's not the man in the club, maybe my feeling's wrong. Maybe Dane's bag lady story is just another random event…just another coincidence.* Even though I still didn't believe in coincidences. And I knew my "feelings" weren't wrong very often.

———————

Not long afterwards, James's new car was parked out front when the sound of another huge crash sent him running, only to find another drunk driver had totaled it.

"Mom, my car!" he said to me sadly. I couldn't believe this had happened again. What are the odds that two of his cars would be destroyed in the same way within three years? And what was it with drunks and my son?

"I think something's got it in for me," he said softly, and a chill ran through me.

I thought about the old witch's prophecy, the one about darkness following me, as I had so many times. Of all the dozens of houses side by side for miles on our street, why did this happen at that exact spot in front of our house, twice? It was more than strange. It was frightening.

"Honey, we'll take all the insurance money and help you get a new one," I told him uneasily. "*And,* we won't park on the street any longer!"

James found a gorgeous SUV with leather seats that he absolutely loved. He felt like he was king of the world, though it cost a lot for his income at the time. We were happy to help, using the insurance money for the down payment. But without the insurance money, we couldn't have.

Two weeks later, James called from the interstate. The SUV had overheated. We checked the water, then drove it to the dealership. They said the engine was fried. We called our mechanic, assuming something must've been wrong with the car.

"Those are extremely difficult to keep cool," the mechanic told us. "That model's so sensitive, it's not a good year for a kid to have." Now they tell us.

Although James had taken great care of it due to his excitement, the dealership said it was James's fault. I didn't believe it, but we had no recourse. Five thousand dollars gone and no money left to buy another car. James bought a bicycle and borrowed my car as much as he could. I promised him I'd try to give him my car as soon as I paid it off. Something had to give; this just wasn't working out well at all. The "darkness" was closing in.

10

Nearing the End

James came bounding in one day full of news.

"Mom, I got a new job at a pizza shop and a new apartment too. I'm moving in with the guys in the band!" His new job was close by, so he could ride his bicycle. That worked for a while.

By this time, I'd eased into a better acceptance of psychic things, but I still went through periods of worry after acting on or using my abilities—it being considered an "abomination unto the Lord." I knew the Bible said prophecy was to be used for "exhortation, edification, and comforting" others. I fought with myself over these definitions and about whether it could be said I was using it this way. When the worry got to be too much, I'd focus exclusively on music for a while. But soon the backlog of people wanting read-ings built up, and driven by my desire to help, I'd return to psychic work. Sometimes, in a downtime, when I was not overtly using abilities much, they came in very strong.

One such time, I got a call from Brian Fain, a friend and the founder of Massillon Ghost Hunters Society, who I'd met a couple years before at one of Sherri's events.

"I'd like to get your opinion on a case we're research-ing right now," he told me. "There's a lot of turmoil in the house and some manifestations we're trying to debunk." A natural skeptic about psychics, he was careful not to give any information about location or evidence involved.

Suddenly some names were spoken inside my head. "I'm getting the name Jerrod for some reason, and the name Jack," I said.

Silence.

"That's the father's name, and one of the son's," he fi-nally answered. "I can't believe you just said that!"

"Well, it doesn't always work that way, but some-times it does. When it's 'on,' it's a bit scary in its ac-curacy." We discussed the feelings I was getting, and I gave him my insight on what I felt was happening there.

Not long after, he called again. "Hi, Debra, we're work-ing on a case, and I thought I'd see if anything came to you. It's a public building and we're trying to track down EVPs recorded there."

EVP stands for Electronic Voice Phenomena, a dig-ital recording of a voice not audible to the human ear, as the frequencies are well below the range of sounds we can perceive. Usually EVPs consist of a word or two, sometimes a short phrase, and are grouped by class; "class A" being clear and understandable upon playback. Other than seeing a full-bodied apparition, EVPs are the Holy Grail of ghost hunting.

"Okay, I'm getting the name Mary right now, and that this place is a library," I said.

Again, stunned silence.

"Wow, the place *is* a library!" He laughed. "Let me grab the file and see if the name Mary has anything to do with the library's past when part of it was a residence. Hang on a minute."

I heard papers shuffling, and another name suddenly was spoken in my mind—*Clare.*

"Here it is," he said, coming back on the line. "Okay, Mary lived at the estate from 1866 to 1880. I'd say that's a direct hit!"

"Hey, I just got another name for you. It's Clare, they called her Clare."

"Okay, hang on." Once again, the sound of shuffling papers. "All right, this is unbelievable. Clara was the woman who lived there after Mary, from 1880 to 1892."

"Yeah, okay, that makes sense," I said. "And, I guess I'm not just reading your mind, since you had to look it up." I was still trying to figure out *how* I knew this stuff.

"No, I didn't even know these names; one of my investigators just finished this report, and this is the first I've seen it," he said.

"Well, this is who's talking on your EVPs—one of these ladies, or both."

Later on, he confessed to me that this was the day he became a believer in psychic abilities. Soon after, Brian asked me to join MGHS.

————

One day James stopped by. He made me put down the paper and listen, so I knew it was serious. He wanted to buy a motorcycle since we couldn't yet pay off my car to give to him. All I could think of was how little he was.

"I don't know, James, maybe something will change and we can help with a car."

But nothing did change, and when he came to me saying he'd found a small bike, a 250 cc, I wavered. My family rode, and I'd had one myself and survived it just fine. I had a momentary flash of the strange "coincidences" that destroyed his cars, but I was trying not to be so paranoid concerning James.

"Let me think about it," I said. I'd begun to trust he'd be okay, to discount the fear for him I'd always had. I did my best to focus on my own life again.

———

As part of my refocusing, I became busier than ever in music—despite the damage from years of Rheumatoid Arthritis. I'd found antibiotic therapy ten years earlier, and it was the miracle treatment I needed to play. But the first twenty years had definitely taken their toll. My fingers were twisted now. Per my usual habit, I ignored the physical realities and hotly pursued music, leaving no room for an empty feeling inside. My life was based on performance and efficiency, which to me, equaled being worthwhile. Somewhere inside, I knew it was neurotic and dysfunctional, but I couldn't stop. I had to feel good enough—like I wasn't just taking up space better filled by someone more worthwhile than I was.

———

One evening I was booked for a psychic party. I'd already done my preliminary readings for the party list, and driving south that night, I opened my mind to receive any last-minute clairvoyant information. I'd turned off the radio to eliminate distractions and cracked the window a little, letting in the thick, green smell of summer. But still I was stuck on one image.

Every time I'd come to one particular woman's name on the list, I'd gotten a strange vision. More like a psychedelic porno movie than clairvoyance! For lack of a better way to put it, it was a "green weenie"—an erect male organ flashing a vivid lime green! As I drove, it was all

I could think of! But what in the world did it mean? I knew I hadn't just dreamed it up; it felt like someone else's thoughts inserted into my head—someone with a very uninhibited sense of humor! Puzzled, I'd written it down under her name. But how on earth could I bring this up to her face to face?

When I finally met her, I was relieved. She was young, blonde, beautiful, and easygoing—so I wouldn't have to worry too much about being "proper" when I explained.

"Hi, I'm Miranda," she said, sitting down at my table.

"Hello," I replied. "I've had some interesting things come up for you." *Oh no*, I thought, embarrassed at the unintended pun. *Why'd I say that!* "Let's see what the cards have to tell you," I said, stalling. I laid out her cards, and could see immediately she'd been through something bad. The ten of swords, a figure face down with ten swords in his back; the Tower, with lightning striking and occupants falling; the nine of swords, a woman in despair, head in hands, swords hanging heavily over her. Despair, catastrophe, and worse. My heart sank as it always does when I see someone's pain. Then pictures started flashing in my head.

"I'm sorry you've been through a really rough time," I began. Her eyes filled with tears, and mine did too.

"Thank you, yes, it's been bad," she said. "I assume you can see that in my cards."

"Yes, I can. But I have something to ask you before we go any further." I didn't want to cause her unnecessary pain so I wasn't sure how to proceed. The "green weenie" vision seemed ridiculous, yet I knew it was important or it wouldn't have been so insistent. *Well here goes*, I thought.

"Um, well first, can you tell me if the phrase 'green weenie' means anything to you?"

Her hand flew to her mouth and she began to cry and laugh at the same time. "Oh my God, look." She leaned down and rolled up the leg of her jeans. There, above her ankle, was a tattoo of a green guitar. "This was my husband's," she said. "He called it 'the green weenie.' It was his favorite. He was a musician and he passed away recently."

"Did he have an irreverent sense of humor?" I asked, in tears myself.

"Oh, that describes him perfectly," she laughed, wiping her eyes.

"Well, he sure got my attention by the image he showed me." I described the picture I saw in my mind. "He must've known I wouldn't 'get it' if he'd just shown me a green guitar." I laughed and shook my head. "I'm a musician too. Maybe that's why he showed me this."

He'd been diagnosed with end-stage cancer, she explained, although at the time he'd seemed in great health. He was the love of her life, her soul mate.

He sent several more messages through me, and she was comforted. We both left the reading wrung out, but glad we'd met. I thanked God for allowing her this little bit of peace.

When tragedy wore a personal face like this, I also thanked God for all my blessings.

————

James kept after me as he always did when he wanted something badly, and finally I gave in on the motor-cycle. He needed my help to get it, and help I did—despite the nagging thoughts about what seemed like the systematic destruction of his three cars. I got the loan and set up insurance, and he made payments.

At first, he loved the bike. He'll be okay, I told my-self. But every time I was out driving and heard a siren or saw police lights in the distance that next summer, I panicked and drove toward them with heart-stopping fear—over and over again. I couldn't shake it. I know now I was being driven psychically to do this. I should have paid more attention...but once again, I didn't.

————

"James, would you like to go on a ghost hunt in West Virginia?" I asked next time he stopped.

"Wow, that'd be fun," he replied.

The West Virginia Penitentiary in Moundsville, just two hours from our home in northeast Ohio, was an in-famous haunted location. It was one of Sherri's events, an overnight ghost hunt, where you arrived about eleven p.m. and were locked in until five a.m. James and his girl-friend sat behind me on the bus, which was equipped with TVs. We watched all the shows filmed there: *Paranormal State*, *T.A.P.S.*, and *Ghost Adventures*.

When we arrived, I made sure the kids were wearing holy water—just a precaution—although James didn't want to.

While James was off exploring the prison, I set my table up in the visitors' room beside the lobby. The room is small, with metal stools and a glass partition on one side, but big enough for my table. The room's huge metal door was open; it must've weighed five hundred pounds. During a lull, I stood up to see if my next reading was waiting. Yawning, I glanced down at my table—and BOOM—the door slammed shut! I felt the tingle begin. I was shut in the room! I jumped, startled, and walked over. Very slowly the door pulled back into place—it was so heavy! I don't think it could've closed on its own, I think something didn't like me there.

A few moments later, James returned. "Mom, check out these pics," he said, showing me the camera. "I'd just walked outside and felt something behind me, so I turned and took this." His picture was of a thick mist, just in front of the door, but it was a clear evening. "And we also took this one." He showed me a strange transparent head coming out of a cell.

"Wow, James, this is intense," I said. "Most people don't get any evidence at all and you got two great pictures your first time." *I hope the holy water keeps him safe*, I thought.

———

James loved his new job and his new place. Growing up an only child sometimes made him long for siblings, and his new living arrangement was about as close to that as you could get. Lots of activity and people—it was party central for a while. He loved his life, even if there were some setbacks. "It's all good, Mom," he'd say often, his favorite line.

I'll never forget those calls at one a.m. when James was broke: "Mom, I'm hungry for toasted cheese, can you bring me one?" Since it was only ten blocks away, I'd make the trek, dropping off his clean laundry with the snack. Despite my effort to let go, I still babied James—I spoiled him terribly. But I loved doing it, and I think he loved knowing I'd be there for him if he needed me.

Ever artistic, James took up painting: cartoons, caricatures, and various scenes. One night, on a toasted cheese and laundry delivery, I was a bit taken aback to see a giant four-by-four–foot painting of a human heart—bloody severed arteries and all.

"James, what in the world!" I cried. He just shrugged.

Soon after, he stopped by our house and played a couple of new songs for me, sadder than his usual hopeful lyrics. "*As close to tortured as I've ever been, is lying here wondering, if my heart might beat away and away and away.*"

The heart painting, and now this? What was bothering him about his heart? He didn't always tell me now. I shrugged off the cold chill as he sang.

That night, I dreamed: James, Dad, and I were going on a very long trip, we were packing our suitcases …

————

"Hey, Mom, I've got a question," James said next time he stopped by. "I'm considering moving to LA in the fall, can I move home to save some money?"

Of course we were okay with it. I was happy to have him back, and he moved in the first of April. He opted for the garage, his old "shed" from younger days. He cleaned it up, and was content.

On my birthday in June, he flew to LA to see his best friend, a pro skater from Ohio. They partied, talked philosophy deep into the night, slept on the beach, and even spent a night with some homeless people, just to hear their stories. When I heard this, I freaked out and called, worried about serial killers and the like. James just laughed at me. He had no fear. He liked and trusted everyone.

At the airport, I searched for him in the crowd, and as he finally came into view, black leather jacket, tousled hair, and crooked smile, my heart ached with love at the sight of him. *I want to remember him like this always*, I thought. He'd only been gone ten days or so, but thank God he was back and safe again. I just couldn't shake the fear.

"Mom, the experience was life-changing, simply unbelievable," he said. "I feel like it's changed me, and I saw things in a whole new light. It really was the best trip of my life."

He told me he'd decided to stay in Ohio, go to college, and just catch a plane when he needed to travel. I was thrilled, and could see he was finally moving into adulthood, maybe a couple years late—just like me. After all, I didn't begin to settle down until I was twenty-five. I'd had to, with my Rheumatoid Arthritis beginning at age twenty-four and five months. James was now twenty-four and three months old; we were on the same schedule.

––––––––––

Although he'd loved his bike, James suddenly seemed spooked by it. He wanted to sell it, and I told him to, and I'd help with a car purchase. After he returned from LA, he rode it as little as possible, and when he had to, he stuck to side streets. He also borrowed my car as often as he could. Sometimes, though, I complained about all the gas he used.

––––––––––

In July I got a call to try to either calm or banish a presence in a house where young children were being tormented by something. I did cleansings occasionally, and often explained to others how to do them. These children couldn't sleep and were scared to be in their rooms. I wanted to help, though I got a bad feeling about it from the start. I loaded up my bag with sea salt, holy water, sage, and all the things I used for a cleansing. GPS showed me the geographic way, and I hoped my gift showed me the rest. I always asked for God's protection, grounded myself, pictured white light surrounding and enfolding me, and applied blessed water.

They were a nice young couple, but the house had a dead, leaden feel to it, and the sensation I got had the quality of "waiting." With the voice recorder on, I asked questions. With holy water, I made the sign of the cross on the walls, doors, windows, and children's rooms throughout, lit sage and fanned it in each room, and distributed the salt, reciting prayers as I went and asking the presence to leave.

It just didn't feel good in there, and it didn't feel much lighter when I was done. Not only that, but the heavy oppressive feeling seemed to come with me when I left. I listened to the recorder to see if any EVPs were caught, but heard nothing. I couldn't shake the ominous feeling. Maybe this had something to do with me. But sometimes a cleansing just made something mad.

———

Back home, James was a blur; staying up all night talking to friends all over the world on instant messenger, typing furiously with one finger as fast as others do with ten. I'd hear him come in for a snack in the early morning and as a night owl myself, this is when we'd talk. He was full of plans, excited everything was finally going his way.

Two new companies asked to sponsor him, and in his promo pictures, he grins into the camera with an expression of cautious disbelief: "Can you believe I'm actually being sponsored to skate—something I love?" His brow furrowed self-consciously and his crooked smile wry, he looks as if he just woke up and as though the pose he's striking is both silly and wonderful.

————————

When Mom died on that beautiful warm April afternoon, we never imagined that by November Dad would be going on a date. He brought the woman he'd met at the senior center to see me play. She seemed vivacious and focused on Dad, but I felt uneasy when she made references to him being handsome and flirting with other women. My dad had never flirted with another woman in my entire lifetime! I watched him, puzzled at the woman's assessment. No flirting. I made a mental note and dismissed it. I realized some families might be upset at such quick involvement following their mother's death. But I was grateful he'd found someone, otherwise I thought he'd die of grief. Mom had been his whole life, he just wasn't used to being alone. He hated it.

Things moved fast from that first date, and although she had different ways, we welcomed her. It wasn't long before Dad seemed pressed to leave his subsidized apartment for senior citizens and move in with the woman. *This is way too soon*, I thought, the rent-controlled apartment the least of my worries. I asked Dad to think it over, since the waiting list for his apartment was three years long. I begged him to give the romance some time.

Dad seemed to understand why I was worried, but he was past the point of caring. As a compromise, just to keep me happy, he agreed to keep his apartment an extra two months after he moved. *That's not long enough*, screamed the little voice inside, but outwardly, I only nodded. James just shook his head after Dad left, knowing my fears.

"He's in love," James said.

Dad told me she'd hung up on his landlord and his female cousin next. "I think she really likes me and is scared others are a threat." He stared off into the distance, a glazed, almost grateful expression on his face.

I flashed back to many years ago when I wore that same expression—of naked, undying gratitude when a handsome man chose me over my gorgeous girlfriends. How wonderful I felt. *Oh no*, I thought, *this is too familiar*. He reminded me of myself.

Not long after he gave up his apartment, trouble started. There were fights, most ending with Dad being asked to leave. Poor, mellow Dad had never experienced so much as a raised voice with Mom. I'm sure he didn't know what hit him.

He'd come to my house, forlornly telling me the terrible things said—things he just wasn't equipped to handle. He'd always been a hard worker, a great husband and father, but not a fighter. I worried about him embroiled in this. He was famous for his even temper and calming influence, so this definitely wasn't his style.

I recognized a control issue, from my own past. Three times after leaving, Dad came to my house very upset, saying he couldn't let it go on. It was destroying his spirit. Each time he'd ask me to find him an apartment…but then be invited back. I'd drop the plans, and cancel with the landlady, sometimes having to get back the deposit. And, in spite of it all, Dad just kept going back. He was lonely. Early on, he'd uneasily asked me not to call their home number, to call his cell instead. That's when I realized that my occasional calls must be causing him problems. I missed him terribly, especially after the loss of my mom, but I accepted it.

Then one day after a particularly bad fight, Dad came over. He was determined to leave this time, he said. Gathering my courage, I repeated what I'd learned from my own experience: the symptoms of these types of relationships. I was exhausted, tired of him changing his mind, but I wanted to help. Once again, I made all the plans for a new apartment. Dad and I looked at it together. I took the deposit over, only to have him call the next day, telling me to cancel.

"Dad, I don't even know what to say! How can I call the landlady and do this to her again? How can you go back and trust things will be any different?" *But you felt just like him,* said the little voice inside, *and only* you *could decide when enough was enough.*

"I love her," he said sheepishly. "She's a good woman, she just loses her temper, I think."

I can't count the number of times he said these words to me.

This time after they made up, he'd spilled everything I'd said about these kinds of relationships. I believe he was trying to put a stop to his problems by making them public, making sure it was understood that everyone now knew.

Soon after, Dad wrote a note, one of several, which I later found in his lockbox:

> "*To my kids, I am writing you to inform you that I am not under any pressure at all living with_____. We have an understanding that I am not to worry about duties of home ownership. I am of such age that death could come at any time and _____ is not to be blamed.*"
>
> —*Dad*

Dad never wrote any notes like this before in his life. To me, it spoke volumes.

I continued to do my best to keep the peace for Dad's sake, but I didn't think his companion could help the behavior any more than my old boyfriend could.

Though Dad seemed to be in denial, I remembered how it'd been for me: how I wanted to fix things, be happy, and a part of something. I remembered all my discounting of psychic warnings and red flags. Denial suddenly seemed to run in the family. Or was it a conscious, willful decision to remain blind to peril, to think nothing bad can ever happen to us?

The years went by, and it felt like I'd lost my father. I rarely saw him. I let go as much as I could and squashed down my growing dread. "Lighten up, it's all good," James said when I worried out loud—providing me more ammunition to discount psychic feelings. Dad loved the hustle and bustle of his new life and family, when it was peaceful. As long as he was happy, I could accept even the loss of him. I didn't want to go down there, and Dad didn't come here often. And when I did see him at my door, I knew it usually meant apartment hunting again. Sometimes James went down to see his grandpa, oblivious or just ignoring it. Maybe James was practicing the family trait too, a generational curse. I kept hoping they'd settle into a peace of sorts, but instead this went on for six years.

We were invited to a cookout there the first of August, and James came down before work, Dad slipping him a ten-dollar bill as he usually did. If you didn't know the undercurrents, it looked like a happy blended family. But it was simply an uneasy truce. I prayed for Dad a lot.

I followed James home on the bike that day, watching his slight figure lean into the turns, laughing as he turned around to grin at me, full of love for him. I wish I could've seen the future this time, for them both. Looking back now, maybe I did see it, but once again, denial took over; denial of the little voice, denial of anything bad ever happening again, and denial of the fragility of life.

————

The second-worst day of my life started out sunny and beautiful. Just like any other day. You'd think a last day would be less ordinary because of its importance. It'd been an ideal summer for skating, the weather cool and dry. James took full advantage, skating eight to ten hours on his days off from the pizza shop.

I left the house about eleven a.m. James had the garage door open and we talked as I passed.

"Good morning, Hon. Did you get something to eat?"

"No, I'm not hungry yet," James answered. "Where're you going?"

"I'm going down to Grandpa's for a few minutes. He just called asking me to teach him how to text." It was an out-of-the-blue request, and I was looking forward to seeing him.

"Oh, okay. I'd kinda like to see Grandpa," he said.

"Well I have a few other things to do, so I won't be back for a while. Love you."

Why didn't I ask if he wanted to come? Later I realized he was out of cash, and could have used the ten his grandpa usually gave him.

Later that day, I was sitting on the sofa learning texting myself, when James came in and leaned over behind me.

"Hi, Hon," I said, not looking up. "Whatcha doin'?"

"I think I'm gonna run down to the skate park for a while," James answered. I was so engrossed in how the phone worked, I didn't pay much attention. James hung over the back of the sofa watching for a couple minutes. I realized later he probably wanted to ask to borrow my car, or maybe a ten, but was reluctant since I'd mentioned taking it easy on gas. Still, I was distracted, so I didn't offer the car as usual.

"Okay, see you later," James finally said, heading for the door.

"Love you," his dad and I called. We'd always done this, and James was never ashamed to say it back.

"Love you too," James answered. The last words he'd ever say to us.

James skated for the next three hours. He swung by the pizza shop to borrow against his paycheck. They asked him to stay, but he said his skater friend was waiting on him at home.

In the meantime, I was on the front porch when James's friend arrived to tell me James was on his way. James had told him to wait in the garage. It was a beautiful end-of-summer evening, just before dusk, August 26.

At some point, Rod noticed sirens close by. I never heard them. I'd been obsessing about my own problems, deep in thought about how to deal with things wrong in my own life. My psychic antennae weren't focused on James—his life was going great. I was the one who needed help; letting go of James and refocusing on my own life wasn't going so great. I was floundering.

Suddenly James's friend came out of the garage on his cell phone.

"Where's James? You've been waiting awhile," I called to him.

"I'm on the phone with a friend," he said. "She says James has been in an accident in front of her house."

"Oh my God, where?"

"Down the street and around the corner," he said.

All three of us jumped in the car. As we turned the corner, my mouth went dry with fear. Down near the end of the street were the flashing lights of police cars and ambulance I'd seen a dozen times in dreams and visions. But I still didn't get it. I still thought everything would be okay, that the darkness could never win.

11

Out, Out
Brief Candle

With my heart in my throat, I, along with Rod and James's friend, rushed toward the lights. *Don't be silly*, I thought— we'll get there to find James on the curb with a crooked smile, shaking his head, with a broken arm or something. Spotting the crowd, we parked and ran to the middle of the street. No sign of James anywhere. The bike lay sprawled on its side a few feet from the curb; a red Firebird was parked askance down further. The ambulance with its rear doors closed sat a few feet from the bike. Glass sparkled on concrete and a large puddle of gas spread out from the bike. We ran to a cop, as the chaplain walked over.

"I'm his mom. Where is he?" I asked fearfully.

"He's in the ambulance; they're stabilizing him," the cop answered.

People lined the streets, staring. I seemed suddenly above myself, not there at all, looking down on it.

"Can we see him?" I asked, unable to see into the high, lighted rear windows of the ambulance. Rod had run over, trying to get in, but he was stopped.

"No, they won't allow you in while they're working on him."

The sense of unreality kept me calm in spite of the chaos.

"They're going to Life Flight him," the cop said. "We don't know which hospital yet. Go straight home and we'll call you."

This seemed ridiculous—not right; my injured son was mere feet away and I wanted to be there. But it was their scene.

"The helicopter is at the fairgrounds," said the cop. "As soon as we know where he's going, you can follow. Go home, wait for our call."

The ambulance pulled away, and with nothing more to do, we ran back to the car.

We'd barely got into the house when the phone rang. "He's going to Akron General," the voice said.

I called Dad and told him to call everyone.

The fairgrounds were only blocks from our house, and I spotted the commotion on the track, the helicopter sitting on the infield. "Rod, they're still there. Maybe we can see him before they leave," I cried.

This could not be happening.

As we pulled in, I saw the ambulance and paramedics near the rear of the helicopter. The cops had told us not to go, that they wouldn't let us near him, but we wanted to try. We ran over to James, strapped on a gurney; they were trying to get an airway down his throat to breathe for him; how small he looked, how still.

"He's out. We put him under; he was fighting," the paramedic told me. The news made me happy—James was tough, wiry, and strong! I thought it was a good sign.

James's feet were bare; I held his sweet feet, one in each hand, sending all my love and energy into him, praying nonstop.

A paramedic looked up at me. "I'm glad you're here," he said. "We're having trouble stabilizing him for the flight."

Uncomprehending, I stared first at him, then at James's face, looking for blood; there was none. He just looked like he was asleep. I could feel the warmth of his bare feet in each hand. My heart ached with love and pain. How could this be?

Finally, they said he was ready and told us they were leaving. We ran back to our car and headed north as fast as we could safely go. On the way, we looked up as the Life Flight passed over us. We watched until it was a tiny speck that finally disappeared with our baby inside.

A crushing weight descended on me—helplessness, fear—and I tried to push it back. I closed my eyes, asking to be shown what would happen—but all that the light formed for me was the picture of a brain. What could this mean? *It means James will be okay,* I told myself uneasily. He'd had broken bones and skating injuries over his lifetime; this would just be a little worse. *He'll be so interested in hearing all this when he wakes up,* I thought—*he'll get a kick out of the flight. He's never been in a helicopter before.*

At the hospital, we were ushered to a waiting room. Soon the neurosurgeon came to speak with us.

"He's got a large section of bleeding on the left side of his brain," he explained, "and there's a clot forming. We have to get this removed, so he's going to surgery now. It looks like the bleeding from the lungs is minor, and he probably has a broken left ankle. There's a large contusion on his back, as well as a small one on the back of his head, and other bruising and scratches. The brain injury is most important right now, so we focus on that first. The ankle and other things we'll get to, but first, we must fix the life-threatening injury." The doctor looked tired and sad.

"Thank you," I mumbled. "We'll be here waiting when surgery is over." I couldn't be hearing what I was hearing. How could it be this bad?

But the doctor seemed so very downbeat and concerned. "He'll be in surgery a few hours," he told us. "We'll open a small section of his skull and leave it open to allow for swelling. The next three days will be critical. He'll be in a medically induced coma for at least two weeks to let his brain heal. The swelling of the brain is what's so dangerous—but I've seen worse than him walk into my office three months later, doing just fine."

Although he was trying to be comforting, the resigned look in his eyes and the severity of his demeanor froze me to my core. Rod and I didn't really understand why he seemed so discouraged, and after he left, we asked each other for opinions on what he'd said, what it meant.

Thirty to forty of James's closest friends packed into that little waiting room that night and every night, leaning against the walls, sitting in the corridors, sleeping on the floor. They wanted to be near him. They truly got us through it. I told the nurses I was sorry there wasn't room for anyone else. They said it was great to see the support, and they sent people who needed a place to wait to another room. This room was ours.

Finally the surgeon came back. "He did well. We got the clot out. Now it's a waiting game to see how much his brain swells from the trauma and the surgery. We'll know in the next two to three days."

We thanked him and asked if we could see James. They led us to the ICU, and there he was, looking like he was just sleeping, though he was hooked to a ventilator. Lights flashing and equipment beeping, Rod took one of his hands and I took the other. *Such warm and sturdy hands, from the time he was little*, I thought, though both his wrists were tied by cloth restraints.

"We're going to let him wake up a little, to see how he's reacting," the nurse said. "He's been sedated since the paramedics put him out at the scene, and given more in surgery, so now we need to let him wake up."

I quickly scanned his body for damage: he was covered with bruises, a bloody cut was on his upper arm, and his left ankle was enormous. Anxiously watching, praying and hoping for the best, we waited. I wanted to talk to James to tell him it would all be okay, to tell him Mom was here with him, just like when he was little and got hurt. My heart ached with love for him, and I would've given anything just to take this on for him. To trade places.

Suddenly, he did the full-body stretch and the little half smile that he did every single time he woke up. He'd done it since he was a baby, and the last time I'd seen it was just few days before, when I woke him in his garage. I leaned in closer, a huge rush of relief washing over me—this was James acting completely normal, as if waking up from a good long nap. I held his hand and bent close to his face. "Sweetheart, it's Mom, we're here with you. Everything's gonna be okay."

He came out of the stretch and further into consciousness—and suddenly his hand began to squirm and fight against mine, his arm pulling and straining against the ties around his wrists—but only on my side; on Rod's side, his hand lay limp. My heart sank. He didn't hear me or understand me; he didn't know what was happening, to fight like this. And his right side was paralyzed from the damage on the left side of his brain. *Oh, God, please help him,* I prayed, *please.*

"He's still combative," said the nurse—this was when I learned that fighting was the sign of a severe head injury.

He'd be safe that night, they told us. And after a lot of questions, we decided to travel home to gather what we needed to stay at the hospital.

We awoke early to newspaper headlines about James, and who'd hit him, and my heart froze. It was the mother of James's old school friend—the quiet young man whose mom was a heavy drinker. Not only had she been almost three times the legal limit, she also had a bag of pot, and a previous DUI. Though disgusted and furious, there was no time to dwell on this.

We swung by the police station to pick up James's backpack, and seeing his skates inside, I understood the contusion on his back. Little by little, the story came out: The neighbor girl on the corner saw it happen. James looked both ways at the stop sign and made a right turn onto the main street, only to be hit by her car cutting the corner, turning into his lane at high speed. He flew almost thirty feet and landed on his back—on his skates in his backpack. I became physically sick. But there was more: the neighbor girl's mom had run out to comfort James, asking if he was all right; he tried to talk, but couldn't form words. He gave one scream, then curled into a fetal position on the street, crying—while the driver sat in her car popping gum to kill the smell of alcohol, according to witnesses. The seeds of my rage were planted.

Most of the next two days, Thursday and Friday, were spent between James's room and the waiting room, greeting people. James was universally loved. We all grew close there, and I know if James could have seen it, he'd have loved it. I went to see him often and put Chapstick on his lips; he hated chapped lips. They'd had to shut off all fluids to him, trying to prevent brain swelling. He still looked almost normal, like he was sleeping, but with a bandage on his head. On Saturday, the third day, this changed.

The worst day of my life began seamlessly. After days with little to no sleep, we'd slept fitfully in the waiting room and very early went to see James. The sight of him shocked us to our very core. His entire head and face had swelled up almost twice its size, so grotesque and distorted I was sickened and knew the worst had happened. There'd been some swelling Friday, but not much, and we'd been encouraged. We waited for the doctors to tell us what we already knew.

"There's significant damage now," they said. "If he survives, he'll have difficulty speaking and understanding. It's as though he's had a large stroke. He'll have substantial deficits and probably be paralyzed on one side at least." The doctor's demeanor was such that I could see he was letting us down easy. "You have to realize there are quality-of-life issues now; his life will no longer be the life he left a few days ago." For my eloquent child, who wanted to be Bob Dylan, being left unable to talk, sing, or even skate would be his worst nightmare.

"Is there anything else that can be done?" I asked. I would've given anything to save him, even my own life. Anything.

"There's nothing," he said, shaking his head, not wanting to look me in the eyes.

He's seen this a thousand times, I thought. *He knows things we don't.* But I still wasn't giving up. Nor would I admit to myself that I just hadn't "felt" James there—in his body—since shortly after his reassuring stretch that first night. He just seemed "gone." Rod, too, felt the absence. I felt cold.

After the doctor left, I watched the monitors constantly—James's heart rate and blood pressure, all of it. Finally, I asked the nurse for the signs of impending brain death.

"What happens is the swelling, having no place to go, starts down the brain stem," she gently explained. "And that's what shuts off breathing and all functions. There'll be an extended period of time where his heart rate climbs higher and higher, as the swelling exerts more and more pressure on the brain stem."

All day and into the evening, I watched as James's heart rate climbed. I don't know if Rod understood what was happening, but I did. But still I prayed—as did thousands. James was the subject of prayer chains all across the country. If his death was God's will, no amount of prayer would help, but still, I held my hands over his head and tried to heal him myself, knowing that if it were possible, my will alone would have accomplished it.

By evening, his heart rate had been over 150 beats per minute for a long time, and I knew it was the beginning of the end. They told us his gag reflex was gone—the start of the downward cascade. I prayed harder. They retested a few hours later and told us it had come back—almost a miracle. *James is fighting!* I thought. We had a small shred of hope.

I went to the waiting room to tell everyone that a miracle had happened, and James was fighting to stay with us. The girls screamed and jumped in circles holding hands. But just as suddenly as it had returned, it was gone again, and something in me died then as well. I was icily calm, disassociated and unable to even cry.

Very late that night, they told us there was nothing more anyone could do, and to go home and get some rest. I relayed the news to his friends; there were a lot of tears, and nonacceptance—for everyone but me. I knew. I accepted, and I was numb. My son had lost the fight, and I'd lost the only meaningful thing I'd ever had.

"If we go home," I asked the hospital staff, "will you call if anything noticeable happens?" Yes, they said, they would.

We drove home in misery, leaving James's frail little body behind. The inevitable had happened. We wouldn't get confirmation until tests were done; but there really was no question about it now. My sweet Jamie, my baby boy, who I could still touch and feel warmth radiating from—and I still loved so much—his very essence was gone.

It was three a.m. when we got home. I went upstairs to try to sleep, exhausted from little rest the past three days, and Rod went into the basement studio. For years, James's band had been recording there, with Rod as engineer, and memories from every corner flooded in, bringing him to tears.

Crying and asking God how He could do this to us, Rod finally talked to James aloud. "James, I love you, where are you, don't leave me."

Rod immediately heard a strange sound and glanced down. There was a crackling noise, like electricity sparking or paper crinkling, and then the shuffling of papers on the table beside him. This was where James always sat when his friends' bands came to record. Rod usually manned the sound board, while James would sit there watching, pulling out pieces of paper to write notes, usually encouraging them with "You can do that better," or " Man, that was great," and giving them the thumbs up.

Rod looked at the papers. "James, is that you?" he asked hopefully. The papers shuffled again, the crackling sound louder. "James, if that's you, I'm so sorry this happened. I need you here, I love you, don't leave me." If James was making these noises, did it mean he was leaving? Neither of us had felt his presence in his body for days, and now Rod felt this was him, saying goodbye, moving away.

The call came right after. It was the nurse. "I noticed a little bit ago, his blood pressure fell to forty, and his heart rate dropped. I believe this was the sign," she said, "that he's gone now."

He couldn't go with us there, I thought. *Our pain held him back.*

"Okay, thanks for calling." Since the night James was hit, some unemotional robot had taken over. The real me was gone, huddled up deep inside myself somewhere.

"The doctor said he'll come in tomorrow, even though it's Sunday, to do the testing necessary to confirm things," she answered. "Try to get some rest and we'll see you here tomorrow at noon."

I was still too numb to even cry. My baby was gone. He was twenty-four years and five months old. How strange; the exact same age I was when I got R.A. But I didn't die—I only lost my dream, even though that was life-changing for me. I know that if when James got to Heaven, he were given the choice to live, but be unable to play music or skate, he would have turned life down.

But for a selfish moment I wish he could've only lost his dreams.

————

The message was sent out far and wide: Sunday at noon the final tests would be performed, to decide if James still resided in his body. A hundred of James's friends met us there, crying, all hope now gone. The doctor called us into a private room and gently told us what we already knew. They asked about organ donation, which James had wanted. It was his way to be giving, but it's hard on those left behind—coordinating how long the surgeons needed with the schedules of James's out-of-state friends who wanted to attend the funeral. Numb and unable to remember anything I was told, I couldn't hold any thoughts in my head.

Monday August 31 at six o'clock the organ-harvesting surgery was scheduled. Rod and I drove up alone to say our goodbyes. At James's side, as I stood holding one hand and Rod the other, he squeezed my hand. A flash of hope surged through me. But the nurse said it was just reflex. Sometimes I wish I'd have told them to continue life support for a couple more weeks, just to be sure. But I didn't, too lost to go against the flow. In the end, James's swelling was gone, so he looked almost like himself. In that little ICU room, with just Rod and James with me, I asked him to go—to God, to the light.

I assured him we'd be okay, even though I lied. I told him we'd brought recordings he'd made to be played while they operated. Somehow, we said our goodbyes. They came for him at six o'clock, and walking away from that room was the hardest thing I've ever done. Believing their tests that said he wasn't alive anymore, when he was warm, when his chest rose and fell, when he'd squeezed my hand. I had to believe God would've stopped this charade if it wasn't meant to be. I had to believe God was in charge now, even though the darkness was closer than ever in my life, and in my mind.

Late that night, they called to say it was over. I knew it meant his body had now died, completely. I understood now why James painted the picture of that giant heart, why his lyrics talked about "*lying here wondering if my heart might beat away and away and away*"—because that's exactly what his heart was now doing; only it was beating away in another man's body. I hoped his spirit soared to God.

———

We were never alone the next few days—local friends, ex-girlfriends, friends from out of state, we all grieved together.

Late Tuesday night I was trying to fall asleep when I heard James yelling in my ear. He sounded frantic, desperate, but I couldn't make it out. *He's still in shock over his death*, I told myself uneasily. *He hasn't yet found his way, or maybe he's trying to get me to help him.* But I couldn't get a fix on it, I couldn't "feel" or "see" anything concerning him. I couldn't help him—a mother's worst nightmare. Filled with horror at his imagined plight, I talked out loud to him constantly, trying to sound calm. I told him to call out for God if he was lost or scared, to watch for the light. I told him to go with God, that we'd see him again soon, and even though I was still lying, I told him we'd be okay. I told him to come back to me when he could, but if he couldn't, that was okay too (another lie). I tried not to think of forever, because forever without James was impossible. It still is. I prayed constantly, desperate to help him, desperate to bargain with God to forgive him if he needed forgiving, helpless to know either way. I hoped he was accepted into God's presence.

On Wednesday night, my cousin and her husband came. We sat on the front porch, talking, while Rod took James's cousin and his best friend to James's old "shed"—they all felt closer to James there. It looked as if James had just stepped out for a smoke: the computer was on, clothes were scattered, skate parts, lyrics, and half-eaten rolls of Smarties lay on the table.

On the porch, while I listened to my cousin talk, I suddenly felt a strange sensation: a warm hand closed around my right ankle and gave a gentle squeeze. I looked down at my bare leg. Nothing was there. I'd begun to tingle all over and wondered what it meant. What was this? I didn't want to seem rude by interrupting my cousin. Moments later, I heard Rod and the boys talking, and once I heard their story, I knew what'd happened.

James had a surveillance camera he'd hooked up above the door to the garage. He'd connected it to a TV inside. He could lie in bed and monitor who was coming. Inside James's shed, Rod had been talking about James, when he noticed movement on the TV: an opaque white shape about the size and height of a man's head, moving and undulating, expanding and contracting in on itself as it moved from the back porch area, down the sidewalk and toward the garage door.

"Hey," Rod said, "what's that?" All of them watched as the shape on the TV drew up even with their door and stopped, as though looking in at them. Then it moved slowly away, down the sidewalk, toward the alley out back. They quickly opened the door, but it was gone.

When they told me what had happened, I realized that when James couldn't get my attention by grabbing my ankle, he went out back to where his dad was. This set the tone for James's visits. We had a certain amount of hope, if not peace. I worried he was stuck or unwilling to move from this earthly plane, confused at his change in circumstance.

———

I wanted to send James off like a rock star, and I know he'd have liked his arrangements. Thursday we had calling hours and the line of well-wishers stretched down the street and around the block—one of their largest crowds ever. From all over the country, they came with their stories of James, many wearing a shirt or piece of jewelry he'd given them. They told how they'd admired the shirt or bracelet, and before they knew it, he'd taken it off and made them keep it. I used to get angry at him for spending his paycheck so quickly. But that night, we heard stories from poor high school kids who'd come into the pizza shop James managed, without the money to buy lunch, and he'd buy it for them. Money meant little to him. Love meant everything.

Don't get me wrong. I knew he was no saint. He could be as ornery, fun-loving, and girl crazy as most twenty-four-year-olds. But always, that gentle spirit showed through. Five ex-girlfriends waited with us at the hospital, praying for his recovery. Whether he'd broken up with them or vice versa, keeping them as friends was crucial for James. We came away with a new appreciation, deeply touched by the love he'd shown others, and the love for him he brought out in us all. We always knew he was special, but now it was obvious just how special he was.

A few friends told us a familiar story: In the living room of his old house, some girls kept hearing a crackling sound in the kitchen. Believing it was James, they talked to him. It was the same sound Rod heard in the studio—an electric crackling. James had visited these girls as well.

After calling hours and a gathering at the skate park, we headed home. As we pulled in front of our dark house, waiting to turn left into the driveway, I saw a light in the upstairs window, like a flame from a lighter. I pointed it out to Rod.

"Look, someone's upstairs, looking around in the dark with a lighter!"

We watched the flame move, bounce, and travel side to side. It was right in front of the window now, and I couldn't believe they didn't see us coming. In a panic, we crept inside the house, ready to call 911. But the dogs were calm, and nothing was out of place, so instead Rod decided to search himself. For a few tense minutes, I waited downstairs by the phone. But there was no one in the house.

"I know it was James," I said. Rod nodded and once again, I went through the familiar litany—"Go to the light, be at peace, we love you, we'll see you soon"— while trying to hide my grief and fear; I could feel James watching us and I didn't want him to be scared.

The funeral went quickly. As we headed out, the line of cars and the motorcycle escort waited while the hearse took James one last time through his beloved skate park. At the cemetery, Rod carried the tiny marble box with James's ashes—"It's all good," said the carving on its side; James's favorite saying. We buried the box and released balloons, watching as they flew into the bright blue September sky. It was over.

12

Life After Death

The kindness of friends and strangers got us through the months after James's death. We went to grief counseling, but there was no release; my tears wouldn't come, only my rage. My rage was boiling over now and focused on the legal system, largely because I felt I could somehow affect or control the outcome. Everything else was so out of my control. Only in private, mostly late at night, I broke down howling like a wild animal at times, racked with sobs and pain like I've never known. This was the pain of a soul destroyed, of hell let loose on earth, a loss too great to be borne. I felt abandoned by God.

Somehow, time passed, in a cold, black emotional vacuum of total devastation those first months. We no longer had any joy in living. I distracted myself to get through each day. I smelled James's clothes, his hats, breathing in deeply the smell of his hair, of him. I made a wall of James's pictures ascending the stairs, then woke most nights to sit on the steps—crying, touching his face. But it was not the kind of crying that gives release; it was the kind that comes from a deep, bottomless pit of grief and I knew it would never end.

We marked no seasons, no Thanksgiving dinner, no Christmas tree or presents; just endless nothingness, plunged in the memories of all the happy years spent with James. My favorite pastime was fantasizing ways to kill *her*—the monster who killed my Jamie—in numerous creative ways that would be most satisfying to me. My violent thoughts scared me, and I knew I'd moved beyond anything I'd ever dreamed I was capable of. Now I knew how normal people are driven to murder. It would be easy to do, and with less remorse than squashing a bug.

Then the killer's mother sent me a card: her daughter would never hurt any of her son's friends on purpose, it said. A scream of pure rage surged up from deep within me. Did she *accidentally* drink to staggering drunkenness, and get behind the wheel?

Three or four times, I watched James's killer walk down the street near my home, my fury building, my restraint close to crumbling as I waited for justice to be served. I had constant flashbacks: James lying in the street, crying in pain while she sat in her car, popping gum to disguise the smell, and no one he knew there to comfort him. She denied this, but witnesses said otherwise. I couldn't stop seeing it.

James had loved all living things. His friends joked about the time he wouldn't let a bug be killed. He caught it and released it outside, saying it deserved to live too. What would he think of my deep, uncontrollable hatred toward his killer? I thought maybe he'd understand.

Then she herself sent me a letter—carefully worded, so as to deny her legal responsibility. It sounded like a twelve-step program—making amends. My fury nearly killed me. We heard her lawyer had required it, hoping to mitigate the damage. Some people in her AA program told us she sat in the corner texting the whole time, not paying any attention. My hatred knew no bounds. She wasn't an alcoholic—I could've felt some sympathy for that. She was just an irresponsible, middle-aged partier hanging on to teenage ways.

I'd lost control and I was afraid. I no longer knew myself or even cared if I died in prison for first-degree murder...or if I died at all. I had become the darkness.

———

Desperately searching for distractions to blunt my grief, even minute by minute, I found myself watching reality shows, movies on demand, anything, just to make time pass, to keep myself from thinking. I was numbly watching a show the first time it happened: the remote on the coffee table in front of me shut the TV off. Dumbly, I looked first at the remote, then at the TV. I grabbed the remote. Both the cable box and the TV were off; that meant the power button was pushed. There was no storm or anything to cause it. "James?" I asked, wanting him to know I'd gotten the message, if he'd done it. This was the first of a dozen times this happened.

I began to see movement and shadows in the living room with me. I'd turn quickly to look, or glance up when it was above me, but I couldn't quite catch it full on. Rod saw it as well, and several times he thought he saw James standing in the hall or the bathroom, just a "slightly darker than air" shadow. When he looked again it'd be gone. He thought maybe he wanted to see him so badly, he hallucinated it. I'm not so sure. Before James's death, I'd never seen this sort of movement here; it'd been years since our "ghost" acted up.

I also began hearing walking overhead, near my bedroom. When I was in my bedroom or the bathroom upstairs, I'd hear footsteps in the attic above me. Then I began to hear soft talking or muttering, even singing sometimes. I told myself it was coming from somewhere outside. But it became stronger and louder, and each time, after checking outside, I was more convinced it was inside. Especially after James's friend stopped by.

Tazz was a crazy, funny kid a few years younger than James. They'd worked together and through their share of party times and seriousness, they'd grown close. I'd heard that strange stuff was happening to Tazz, and I wanted to know more.

"It's pretty weird," he began. "I didn't really believe in spook stuff before, but I've changed my mind."

James's was the first death Tazz and his friends had been through, the first time they'd had to face their own mortality. If James could die—quirky, funny, larger-than-life-James—then anyone could.

"Tell me what happened."

"Me and a couple friends were in my basement, where I live when I'm at my dad's house. I fell asleep on the couch and woke up when I felt something. My friends across the room were holding onto each other, looks of terror on their faces—they said a blue light had suddenly showed up and was hovering over me, and when they yelled, it shot up the wall and disappeared!"

From my experiences, I knew the blue coloration usually meant a good energy or spirit.

"Then a few days later, as I was sitting in the recliner, I heard a sigh, right over my shoulder. I turned toward it, and it did it again!" I could see his disbelief warring with his new experiences. We both knew that James gave those sighs all the time.

"I'm also hearing humming," he went on. "It's usually somewhere farther off, and it sounds kinda like James." I nodded. It was the same thing I'd been hearing. *At least James seems happy*, I thought, *and still loving music*. We reminisced a little before he left, and I told Tazz to let me know if anything else happened.

Despite the evidence around me, I was afraid to try to get EVPs—afraid of what I might hear. James asking for help would drive me completely crazy. And it would be a short drive.

———

There was no way could we go back to work yet, but living on half pay—Rod's disability/family leave—was difficult. Since I was self-employed, I received nothing. Finally, after more than two months, we had to try. James's friends had organized a benefit to help with our expenses those two months, and contributions were made at several of my regular venues where I'd been performing for years. They sent the money to me at home. It was truly appreciated and had gotten us through to this point. But I needed to try to somehow go on. I really didn't care if I ever sang again; I'd lost all joy and couldn't imagine doing it, but I also knew James would hate it if I quit because of him. I honored this thought more than anything else. And we needed to pay the bills.

I picked the easiest places first—places where there was the least chance of anyone bringing James up. Though it was difficult to imagine going back to performing for an audience, I picked the gigs that mostly strangers would attend—tourists who knew nothing about the loss of my son. Luckily, living in a very high tourist area helped in this endeavor; I simply took gigs offered at those venues over the local ones where everyone knew me. For those few hours of performance, I could put on my "game face" and pretend it hadn't happened. After all the years of "the show must go on" mentality, it came naturally. But if someone took me aside to offer condolences, the façade shattered, the tears came up, and I was done. When I spotted any such well-intentioned folks headed my way, I fled. But I was well known in my area, and they were everywhere: from gigs to grocery stores—I hid out and wished I could disappear.

———

One day as I dragged myself out of bed and into the bathroom, my little dog Bobo came bounding up the stairs.

"What are you doing up here?" I leaned down to pet him, wondering how he got the door open. Both dogs' kennels were in the mud room off the kitchen; that's where they slept. I walked downstairs and sure enough, the kitchen door into the living room, the one we all used, was standing open. The kitchen had two doors at right angles to each other—one opened into the living room and one into the foyer. Maybe Rod had left it open that morning.

"You stay down here, baby," I told Bobo, closing the door. I went back upstairs and finished getting ready. Later, I came down the front steps into the foyer to get the mail out front, then opened the door to the kitchen. As I stepped into the kitchen, I looked at the door that opened earlier, a few inches to my left, wondering how Bobo had done it. While I was looking, the doorknob made its distinctive sound—a metallic click—as it turned and the door slowly swung open.

"James, is that you? Is that how Bobo got in? Are you opening the door? You've got my attention, honey." I told him to keep it up if it was him, but also added the "go to the light" stuff, for good measure.

————————

You might think that such visits made me happy, but I was afraid for him. I remained despondent, and as my worry that I was somehow responsible for James's death escalated, I searched out a priest online. Maybe I could ask some questions anonymously via email and find some comfort or clarity. Although I'm not Catholic, ever since my early days of the haunted house, I've felt an affinity for the religion. After all, the Catholic Church was the only church to truly understand evil personified. They accepted the reality of demons, possession, and all the rest of it, and had tools in place to deal with it. They alone might be able to provide either peace of mind or insight. I wanted to know about these "gifts" I was given. Were they good, or evil? What exactly was I to do with them? Could I have let something in or made myself and James a target just by having them? I'd studied on my own all these years, now it was time to go to the experts.

The online priest seemed kind, answering promptly. I described the nature of my gifts, how I used them for others, and my concerns. I said nothing about my son or my fears surrounding his death. I said only that I wished to understand once and for all what it meant to have a gift like mine and how I should be using it.

"There are two kinds of revelation the Catholic Church believes in," he wrote, "public and private."

I learned that my kind is considered private, and therefore apt to be corrupted by our own faulty human understanding. I already knew this to be true from trying to "interpret" the information I got in readings. I'd learned to interpret as little as possible.

The priest quoted St. John of the Cross as well as St. Teresa of Avila, so I looked them up. I learned that many Catholic saints had clairvoyance and other so-called psychic gifts; some had terrible trials, such as poltergeist phenomena, which they believed were demons, tormenting them as well.

But I'm no saint, so I couldn't imagine what this meant to my life. The gifts ran in my religious family, which made me wonder if being religious somehow earned it for them—with me acquiring it by default? The only thing that really resonated was the St. Teresa quote: "With extraordinary gifts come extraordinary trials." Teresa of Avila was tormented throughout her life, and she had extraordinary psychic gifts. *Well, I've surely been tormented*, I thought. Though the Bible says to desire prophecy above all things,

St. Teresa basically says *not t*o ask for it because it's going to bring you torment.

This shed a whole new light on the subject. Did it simply mean that if you have a gift from God, that those opposed to God will hate and attack you from the outset, more than the non-gifted person? What a terrifying thought…especially since I never asked for psychic abilities.

The priest asked if I wanted to meet, and I decided to. He was young, and we sat in the rectory dining room, the sun streaming through the windows and making patterns on the table.

"Thank you for meeting with me, Father. I'm at a loss to understand what I should do. This isn't something that's just come up. I've struggled with it all my life. Lately, it's really bothered me."

"Well, we believe that what you describe is one of the spiritual gifts," he said. "A gift of the Holy Spirit. I assume you've been baptized?"

"Yes, I guess you could call it that. It was at a lake during a Methodist Church camp for teenagers, and was very informal."

"This is very scary stuff," he said. "You have to be concerned about being misled, or of trivializing the gift, thinking you're doing something for God, when instead you're being sucked further into darkness."

"That's exactly what's scaring me," I told him. "I try to stop, but people call and need help and I want to help them. I feel I was given this gift for some reason, and I want to do good with it."

I explained that I used to worry about something evil causing my gifts—although since I now *prayed* for the information to help people, I no longer thought this was the case; I assumed prayer determined the source of the information I received. I also constantly wore holy water. I gave him examples of how the psychic abilities worked, of the precognitive dream I had of Princess Diana's death, as well as other examples that helped people. Mom always said when prophecies are from God, they always come true; that's how you knew. That's why I thought this was a divine gift, its accuracy pointing to its source.

"I've recently had some personal tragedy and I'm afraid I somehow invited it by allowing this into my life," I continued. "But I don't have much choice, or maybe I should say I was never given a choice. I was born with it." And suddenly I realized how strange this must sound to him.

"I don't think his guardian angel could've stopped a car from hitting him," said the priest—and I realized he was talking about James.

Wow, I didn't see that coming, I thought. *Somehow he knows what happened to James; it's a small community, I guess.* I sat stunned, digesting this.

"You have to wonder why God would give this to you," he suddenly said. "If the information you needed to get out was so important, God would give others with the gift the same information and they could relay it." His tone had turned stern.

Again, I sat, digesting this. What was he getting at? Did he think I was pretending to have this to be important? My heart sank. Maybe I'd failed to impart to him the depth of my self-torment. Somehow my "specialness" of being singled out for this gift had become the issue. This was so far from my reality that my eyes began to well up; I felt hurt, misunderstood, and ashamed, yet again. I needed a spiritual advisor, and didn't realize it might come down to a question of whether it was real or not; I had a hundred witnesses who'd attest to that. But of course he didn't know me. He also didn't know that I got more attention than I needed in my music career; I didn't need any more. What I needed was help, and peace.

"My advice is to be very cautious in using this," he went on. "I wouldn't do readings, I'd avoid working for psychic hotlines or anything of that nature. I'd only use this gift if I felt compelled by God to do so, if information came at the moment you're with that person, to save them from harm."

I nodded, head down, hoping he hadn't seen my tears, hoping I could get out of there soon, embarrassed at my foolishness for going, ashamed again of being just too different. Long ago I'd accepted that my wish to just feel normal would never happen, but it still made me sad every time I came up against it.

"I do feel compelled," I explained again. "I've tried to stop, but people call me and I want to help if I can…" I drifted off. He didn't answer and I knew that was my cue to go.

"Okay, thank you," I said as I stood. "I'll stop doing readings and only give warnings if very compelled. Thank you again for seeing me." He said goodbye, and as I hurried out the door, it struck me—thirty-odd years earlier at the old witch's house, this was exactly how I'd felt. The priest and the witch represented both ends of the spectrum, with me in the middle trying to find my way. It wasn't the priest's fault; no one could understand what I was dealing with.

———

I'd already stopped the readings. I hadn't done any since James died. People emailed, texted, and called, but I made excuses—I was backed up and would get to them soon, I was too busy, whatever. I even raised my prices, thinking it might discourage them or at the very least, I would earn a bit more for losing my soul!

The pain of losing James was always there, but through my technique of distracting myself, I could get it to settle into a dull ache. But there was a nagging, ever-present feeling of something missing, something wrong.

One evening, while alone in the house, settled in on the couch with my laptop, I kept hearing a faint scratching sound at the kitchen door—the same door that had opened up on its own. The door was over my right shoulder, closed, as usual. James's black Lab Leia was in there, but she was usually asleep on the throw rug on the far side of the kitchen, yards away from the door.

Scritch, scritch, scritch. Pause. *Scritch, scritch.* Pause.

Finally, the sound registered, gaining my full attention. *Maybe she moved closer, up against the door,* I thought. I looked around at the door, puzzled. Suddenly there were five loud, rapid knocks on the door, and the old metal doorknob rattled, not three feet from where I sat. "Rod?" I asked, thinking he'd come home. No answer. *It must've been Leia, somehow nosing at the door.* Immediately I heard Leia get up on the far side of the kitchen, the sound of her toenails on tile unmistakable, traversing the fifteen feet from her favorite spot on the throw rug. *It wasn't Leia! She's nowhere near the door!* I heard her stop just on the other side, as though looking up at someone standing there.

"James, is that you?" I called out. I came around the back of the couch and opened the door to Leia standing just on the other side. Nothing there.

"Leia, who is it, girl?" I asked softly. "Is it Jamie?" She stared at me. I couldn't feel anything. Puzzled, I looked down at the doorknob and what I saw took away my breath. Just beside it, on the flat molding of the solid old oak door, were two initials scratched: JS.

"Oh, Jamie, did you just do this?" I cried. "I've never seen it before, honey. Was that you scratching it in? Was that you knocking to get my attention, so I'd notice it?

I love you so much, honey, I miss you, I'm here and I'll always watch for you if you want to come see me."

But if it was him, he was gone now. And I felt nothing.

With tears in my eyes, I went through the usual spiel, telling him to ask God to help him, to watch for the light, that we loved him and would see him again someday. That I was sorry this happened to him, that I was sorry for anything I did that led to it, that I was sorry the doctors couldn't save him, that I'd give anything to have him back, even my own life. I wanted to die.

———

I eased back into playing, focusing exclusively on music instead of readings. Since I'd been to the priest, I felt differently about doing them—way more worried.

One night, almost two years after the psychic party where I'd seen the testicle lump for her fiancé Evan, I ran into Sarah, the young waitress I'd been friends with. I'd lost touch with her, and now we each had terrible news. Evan had been killed in a car wreck just a few months before, she told me. And then I told her about James.

"Evan was having a lot of problems right before the wreck," she told me. "He was bleeding from inside and feeling sick and weak." I immediately thought about the lump and wondered if he was taken quickly to spare him a death by cancer. Sarah mentioned this just as I was thinking it. She'd wondered the same thing.

She cried over his loss. We both cried. She and Evan had a two-year-old boy together—the baby boy I'd seen before she knew she was pregnant—and though I was scared to do it, I promised her I'd try to "see" something for her about Evan. I figured this was as good as being "compelled," in the priest's words. Sarah had been through tragedy and I wanted to help her.

The next day, I took a deep breath and spoke aloud: "Evan, if you can hear me, Sarah misses you so much. She needs to know you're okay and if there's anything you want to tell her." I closed my eyes and waited. Suddenly, I heard a voice in my head and felt a rush of worried feelings. The voice said something about Skeeter, about leaving "Skeeter" behind. I didn't know their son's name, and I was afraid to text Sarah, in case it brought up painful memories. But finally I decided this was too important.

"Who is Skeeter?" I asked when she called me back.

"Oh, dear God, Skeeter is a pet name Evan called our son!" she screamed. "What did he say?"

He was very worried about leaving his boy, I told her, and she assured me she loved their son dearly, would protect him with her life, and she'd always tell him about his daddy. After we hung up, I spoke that message aloud to Evan, and I felt a peace descend on me. I believe he heard me. He was a nice boy and I wish him peace and light, until his young son joins him again someday.

Once again, I'd been pulled back into the psychic world by wanting to help someone. I only wished I could help myself, but James's communications with me continued to be maddeningly elusive.

———

I was sitting on the sofa one night in my favorite pose—TV on mute, laptop on my knees, and feet on the coffee table in front of me—when I heard it: a *thump* from the carpet in front of the coffee table, as well as a slight crackling noise from the ceiling. More curious than frightened about strange happenings since James's death, I looked up just in time to see a small white feather, floating down. I walked around to the front of the coffee table, and there lay the tiny feather on the floor. Nothing else. *What in the world is going on here?* I thought. *This is getting bizarre.* How could a feather fall out of the living room ceiling, or out of anywhere in the living room? It was just so ridiculous, I couldn't believe there was any other explanation but that James was behind it again.

I longed for him so badly. I missed every single thing about him. My frustration at feeling he was trying to communicate but seemed unable to do so on any level ate at me and I feared hearing anything new from him, while also craving it. My mom never came back at all; I think she went straight to God, as some do. Why couldn't I "get" from James the same kind of information I got for others? Was he still not strong enough, not well-versed enough on the other side? Or was it just like it'd always been—when I needed the abilities to do something for me alone, forget it. Then the light bulb went off and I remembered two things that made perfect sense with the feather incident.

The first memory was of my mom and grandma's dream: just before a family member passed away, they dreamt of a white bird; white birds had white feathers.

The second was the day of my mom's graveside ceremony: We'd all sat in folding chairs on a warm spring day, just the closest family members. Suddenly I'd noticed a small white feather floating down from the sky, nearly in front of us. We were in a large clearing with no trees or birds. Though it'd been four years, the memory was still clear. I'd shaken my head, amazed and confounded, and I'd whispered to James, beside me. "Did you see that?" He nodded.

There's a paranormal name for things of this nature: an apport. All kinds of objects can appear in various places, sometimes moved from one room to the next or appearing out of thin air, and this is one explanation for the feather. Once again, there are no definitive answers. But James had an affinity for feathers; I remember him running in with a beautiful full-length hawk's tail feather. I still keep it on the mantel. He told me it'd dropped out of the sky right in front of him and that Native Americans believed a feather was a gift from God. James alone would know I'd remember this. James alone would understand that I'd grasp the significance when it floated down right in front of me, just like the feather in his story. But feathers weren't James in the flesh. They weren't even James's words, which I'd have settled for. And my craving for both was bottomless.

––––––––

After having seriously come close to quitting, I realized that for me, besides James, there wasn't much I loved more than performing. With James gone, it was really all I had. And even after a lifetime of countless gigs, when it was good, it was really good. In fact, after the first rough spell, it became the only time I could forget the pain, so I completely immersed myself in it. To be a good singer, you must access inner emotion, and at first, all I could access was grief. But James had loved playing so much himself, and I wanted to play for him.

When performing is combined with picturesque surroundings, God and nature seem one. This is the situation at one of my favorite venues. A beautiful outdoor setting where people sit on a lawn overlooking a small, tranquil lake, it's my most calming place.

Sitting in a shelter facing the audience, I sang. In front of me was a serene valley, lit by a low-riding sun, an hour from sunset. After so many years performing, I've learned to sing and play while enjoying scenery, people-watching, even thinking about other things. It's a kind of musical autopilot.

I was enjoying the valley, the ducks walking in a line to the lake, and the sound and feel of my voice hitting the notes, when I noticed a shadow off to my right, standing still just this side of a birdbath twenty yards away. As I continued to sing, I watched it. Slightly dense and gray, a little darker than smoke, yet see-through, it was roughly the shape of a man. It was still sunny, and it was strange to see a freestanding shadow in the open where nothing could've cast one. The feeling I got was of peace; there was no tingling warning. For a moment, I watched, my mind registering what shouldn't be there. I turned back to the audience to see if anyone else had noticed it. Only a split second later I looked back, and now the shadow was standing four feet from me at the railing.

Slightly alarmed, only because it'd moved so fast and was obviously watching me, just as I was watching it, I stared. As I sang, staring at it, the shadow stayed put, apparently enjoying the music. No one else seemed to notice. Coming to the end of the song, I turned away from it to acknowledge the applause, and when I turned back, it was gone.

This wasn't James; somehow I just knew this. I believe it was a close friend of the family, the owners of the property, who'd passed away very suddenly, not long after James. I believe this friend simply stops by to check on things. He noticed me, and I think he knows now that I could see him, as he could see me. But once again, the frustration arose. I wanted *James*, I needed *James* to come back like this, in some tangible form. Just a couple words from him would do it—that he was okay, that what we'd always believed of God and heaven were true, so I'd know for sure that we'd be together again someday. That's all I wanted from him. Then I could wait. Then I could go on.

———

Tap, tap, tap. I woke to the sound of tapping. Slowly surfacing through layers of sleep, I heard it again; coming from the table on the far side of the bed. There was a little plastic bear-shaped bottle there, filled with multi-colored layers of sand. James made it at one of the festivals we'd taken him to as a boy. I was wide-awake now. I got up on one elbow and looked at it. It didn't move. There was nothing on the table but a lamp and the bear. The sound had been of plastic and grains of sand bouncing against it, tapping on the tabletop. "James?" I asked. Nothing.

I flopped back down in the bed. There'd been many times I'd smelled the distinctive, one-of-a-kind garage/shed smell in my bedroom, and again I smelled it now. Since the bear was a gift from him, it made sense that he might use it to get my attention. *Dear God*, I thought, *enough with the tapping, James, I hear you! Just come back to me and let me know! Answer my questions, tap your answers, one for yes, two for no.* This tapping and these small yet obvious visits made me think he was crying out for help, but didn't know how else to get through to me. I tried to drift back off again and was almost asleep when the floor began to creak. It started at the door and came all the way up to the side of my bed; a series of creaks that sounded as though someone was walking toward me. Opening my eyes, I searched the space beside me and thought I could feel James there. Again, nothing. But I could smell the garage. "I love you, James. I can't understand what you need, and I don't know what to do." I was near tears. I wanted to "see" him! Why couldn't psychic abilities at least help me do that? "Please, God, help him," I prayed out loud—if it even *was* him. "Please." I was helpless.

13

Now Voyager

The day of the sentencing finally came. I stepped out of the car and took a deep breath, dreading it. Across the alley, not twenty feet away, was the door to the basement of the bank where my baby shower was held; catty-corner to that was the funeral home where I'd last seen James; their parking lot was a favorite skating spot for him. Displayed before me were pages from his birth, life, and death. And now I had to wrap up the final chapter.

I read my victim-impact statement to the full courtroom and the woman who'd killed James. I already knew there'd be little justice—she'd plea-bargained for eighteen months in prison and six months in a halfway house because it wasn't a "violent" crime. *Tell that to James*, I thought. Was this all James's life was worth? Ohio law provided a maximum of eight years in prison for this. I was sick about it.

I said my piece, my insides churning, seething with outrage and a burning, bottomless hatred for this woman, but I knew I'd have to learn to live with this rage … or it would kill somebody. She sat there staring straight ahead. Not a tear, stone cold. No remorse.

When I got home, I ran straight to the bathroom, sick. Each day I got sicker. After being in bed a week, I finally went to the ER. This bottled rage had almost killed *me*.

After another week in the hospital on antibiotics, I went home. They told me this could've been my end, and I also knew that James wouldn't want that. Somehow, I had to let the rage go. I didn't think I could. It was deep, it was visceral; it felt part of me now.

————

Back home, I recovered slowly, and strange things kept happening in our house. Electric crackling noises woke me, shadows moved in the downstairs rooms, the TV turned itself off, and there were sounds of a human voice, sometimes a cough, or a familiar clearing of the throat— just soft enough that I couldn't tell if it was James. I felt him there and smelled his one-of-a-kind garage-room smell. There were gentle touches on top my head while I was sitting on the couch. Rod also experienced this. James did this often when he was alive. But I couldn't get any concrete messages, not the kind I got for others. *Why can*

I do this for them but not for me and my son? I wondered. Between frustration and rage, I teetered on the edge. I continued to tell James—if he could hear me—to go to God, begging God to help him. But God was quiet.

————

The day after the sentencing, Dad turned eighty. Immediately following my own hospital stay, he'd had a series of hospital admissions that left him very weak: he could barely walk.

During the previous six years, I'd seen Dad maybe a dozen times, so I didn't realize that when he got sick his companion expected me to take over his care. I was grieving James, regaining my own health, and by Dad's (and her) choice, not much a part of their lives any longer. One day while visiting Dad in the hospital, I was shocked to be accused of not taking enough responsibility for my father. I'd bowed out gracefully years before, after intuiting it was required of me. After all the years I'd been so close to my parents, I'd lost my dad through no fault of my own. Indignant over the accusation, I saw red, and told her what I thought of her in very few words. I regretted it almost immediately.

Since James died, I'd lost the sociability and tact daily life required. My entire life, truth was always most important to me, though I'd had trouble sometimes "filtering" truthful comments in keeping with my family mediator role. Since James's death, it was as though there was no filter at all. Grief does funny things to a person. And now I'd really done it.

Life returned to my "new depressed normal" for several weeks. I took Dad to doctor's appointments and called often to check on him. Now that I knew it was okay to be involved in his life again, I welcomed the distraction. Maybe I'd finally let off a little of the steam threatening to crack me in two. But it wasn't long until Dad was readmitted for breathing problems.

When ready to be discharged, Dad was too weak to go home without nurses' aides to help him. I'd set the aides up, but when I stopped by, Dad said they weren't allowed to come because his companion thought they would "steal her blind." I argued that they were screened by their companies, and he agreed, but told me he couldn't convince her otherwise. And that's when the full implication of what was happening hit me. I'd suddenly been designated as his helper by default. Maybe she didn't want to be another man's nurse. But I wish she'd have thought of this in the beginning, before Dad left his apartment and moved in with her. She'd also had some health issues of her own, so maybe she felt justified.

"What are you gonna do?" I asked. "You can't even walk!"

"I know. Let me bring it up one more time," he said. "So she understands I'd have to move out if they can't come help me."

He looked sad, resigned, and fragile. Like a lost little boy. This was a terrible blow to his ego—I think he realized then that his unwavering loyalty, even over his own family at times, wasn't reciprocated. Dad had nursed Mom to the very end. He believed it's just what you're supposed to do. That undying blind loyalty again; *that's probably where it came from in myself.* I wanted to comfort him; it didn't occur to me then, but I needed some comforting over all this myself.

I continued to worry over Dad, his health, his hurt. I hoped his companion was just mad at me and at the turn of events, that I was wrong about my conclusions. Dad hoped that she just didn't understand. But after their "talk" the results were the same.

"Well, *now* what are you supposed to do?" I asked him.

"I want you to look for an apartment for me," he answered. "Call my old landlady and see what she has."

I felt sick. *Here we go again,* I thought. *Please God, not now. I just can't take this anymore.*

Dad was allowed to stay with his companion until he could get moved out, but he was so weak he couldn't even get up. My heart sank when he told me he couldn't get himself a glass of water, and was too afraid to ask for one.

Somehow I had to try to fix this. And despite my frayed state of mind, it was all up to me, alone.

I couldn't help him with a place to live. When Mom got sick, they'd sold their house and moved in with me, but Dad was healthier then, easily managing the stairs. We grew even closer during their stay (another reason I was upset by the accusation of neglect). After one of the last times Dad was asked to leave, I invited him to my house again. After stumbling down the stairs from my bathroom, he tripped on the rug and fell through the plate-glass window on the back door. Luckily he wasn't cut badly, but we both realized then that the arrangement wouldn't work.

Finding Dad an apartment wasn't easy. His old landlady was wary of him backing out again, so I cosigned, guaranteeing I'd pay the year's rent if he left, hoping it'd end the charade of him going back over and over. I told him about my investment: if he left, I'd have to pay five thousand dollars.

I set everything up for Dad—within three days. It was stressful. But I loved him and he needed me now. And it did provide some distraction, postponing the agony of James's loss until I was alone, late at night.

I wanted to be done with all this drama. Mom would be rolling in her grave over it, and Dad's involvement in it. It went against everything she'd drilled into us since childhood: "Our kind of people don't do this and don't do that."

At first, Dad was happy in the apartment. It was so peaceful, he said, and he didn't have to worry if he spilled a crumb on the floor. But he missed his old life. He'd never fully grieved Mom's death, having filled her place so quickly. He'd barely been alone a few months.

"All I can think about is Kathryn," Dad said one day.

I went into therapist mode. "The grieving process starts right where you left off," I told him. "You're feeling what you never felt since six months after Mom died." I hoped he understood it'd get easier.

I stopped in every day as Dad got stronger. One afternoon I visited and promised I'd return with dinner. "Please don't," he answered.

"Why not?" I asked. I was finally growing close to him again after six years apart.

"She's coming tonight," he explained sheepishly. "And she doesn't want to run into you."

Hurt flooded me. I hurt from losing him for the past six years and from not feeling appreciated as the only person who wanted to help him. Not to mention the hurt from losing James. I needed Dad after James's death. I know Dad missed James too, but he believed that I just somehow had to get over it, which I couldn't do.

Dad had moved on so quickly after Mom—six months—though he still cried if she was brought up. I guess the companion gave him strength, and he was too fragile to grieve alone. *It sure sounds good to just get over it,* I thought. But I understood now, that for me anyway, it was impossible. I was buried—at the bottom of an endless pit of grief. If Dad grieved for James, he did it alone—as did I.

I began to look at my family in a different light. Nothing was quite as I thought it was, or wished it to be. Maybe there were many things our family had just "gotten over" without really feeling them. Maybe we just swept them under the rug. I guess it was our way. Maybe I was the one who'd always felt, spoken, or acted out the truth in my family. And maybe that, in its own way, isolated me in my family just as much as psychic abilities ever did with the rest of the world.

———

It was inevitable. Dad told me that his companion missed him now that he'd moved out for good. *Oh no,* I thought.

"I just want to be happy," Dad said sadly.

I didn't know what to tell him, but I was afraid he might want to move back in. How would I take care of all his business the way things were between us now? He also didn't have the five thousand dollars for the year's lease. Would she pay that? I couldn't really afford it.

So be it, I thought. If this happened, I'd probably have to wash my hands of it. I wasn't going to take any more, and I wouldn't allow Dad to either. Since I was the one responsible for Dad's affairs, it'd be rough, but if he decided to go back, let the chips fall where they may. I was angry at him—and her—though I never let on.

You're being selfish, screamed my inner punisher, feeling guilty about my anger. I'd always been the "fixer" of the family, but now I needed someone to fix things for *me*, and there was no one. I focused my rage on the companion; every time I thought of her, my heart would race and my rage would rise to the surface at the injustice of it all—and somehow it got all wrapped up with her denial of all the years I'd cared for my parents, with James's death, and his killer and her sweetheart of a plea bargain deal. I was a mess.

————

"I'd rather kill myself than go into a nursing home," Dad told me after his ulcer flared up.

I didn't understand this, especially since they were such nice places. He was getting to that point, and it eventually happens to us all. I don't know what else he thought would happen.

No plans to move back in with the companion were ever mentioned, but he seemed to be slipping from adulthood to petulant childhood, angry at the world, blaming everything except what put him in the now-hated apartment.

I, too, was slipping—deeper and deeper into a formless black rage; at Dad for putting me through it at my most vulnerable time, at being left to deal with it alone, at the killer of my precious son, at God for allowing all this to happen, and finally that James couldn't come back to me any clearer than he had. I was rage personified—even raging that my own psychic abilities had deserted me when I needed them most—to help myself. There was no help anywhere. I was on my own, and truly consumed by darkness.

————

Dad sank into a depression over the loss of his new "family." He still saw the former companion occasionally but apparently, things weren't the same. I made a doctor's appointment for him. There, Dad told the story—how he'd had to leave his home—and the doctors instructed me to take him straight to the mental health center, where again he told the whole story. The nurses and counselors asked what had transpired to cause his suicidal thoughts, and they sympathized. It was sad to see a man this age going through this.

It was sad for me to see his grief over a loss that, to me, seemed the best thing that could ever have happened to him. It was never going to get any better there. Just what'd he think would happen the next time he got sick? The same thing I assumed. Why couldn't he see this? It seemed a clear case of all the eggs into the wrong basket.

They prescribed antidepressants, and though he didn't want to, I begged him to try counseling, and scheduled the first session. He kept saying he felt really bad inside. Dad had been with Mom since he was seventeen, and very happy. I believe, until this age, he'd never experienced the pain of a failed relationship.

I invited Dad for roast beef Thursday, but he was feeling bad, so I took him a plate and sat with him while he ate. His eyes were huge and haunted. My eyes probably looked about the same by this time.

For me, it was a lifetime of things—psychic abilities, the haunted house, the abusive relationship, my health, my job, my son, my dad, everything. Even the tiniest extra thing was too much: Dad needing to be taken to his doctor's appointments, or trips to the ER at six in the morning when my R.A. was at its worst without enough sleep. The fact that I had no help, no one to share the burden of Dad's care during this overwhelming time in my life, pushed me to the breaking point. Until finally one day, home alone, I broke.

"Bring it on you b****rds!" I screamed. "What else you got? I can take it! I'll never turn from God no matter what you do!" I felt I was addressing the personification of evil, the "darkness" that'd followed me for so long and set all this up. I'd decided maybe it was a battle for my soul. But you should never challenge darkness...

I really thought I couldn't take anymore. Until I found out that, actually, I could.

———

Every Saturday, Dad went to breakfast with his new "family," his female companion and at least one of her children and sometimes their families. He looked forward to it so much he'd cancelled his meal deliveries to go. This Saturday, he'd gotten a haircut to look his best, and he waited. They didn't come. He should have seen this coming, but then again, this was an eighty-year-old man who'd been with Mom for over fifty years. Just a few days before, like a little boy defiantly proclaiming his independence, apparently Dad confessed that he'd smoked a cigarette, something that he wasn't supposed to do and that she hated. He said it had caused serious anger.

"Why'd you have to tell her about that, Dad?" I asked. He just shrugged. "No one's answered my calls for a couple days," Dad said forlornly. And now, being stood up for breakfast, it was too much.

————

I was involved in a big meeting that Sunday, coordinating the upcoming skating benefit. Sunday evening, on my way to the cemetery for my weekly visit, I called Dad. "How're you doing?" I asked.

"I feel really bad," he answered.

Why didn't I tell him I'd be right there? Or asked if he wanted to come over? These are thoughts that plague me still.

"Did you get to see her today?" I asked.

"Yes," he replied. "And I went for a long drive."

So he went on the drive alone, I thought. *He saw her, and left. Wonder what happened…*

"Aw, Dad, I wish I could help you. I think it'll just take time. Maybe some trips to the senior center with your old friends will make you feel better." Then I had a momentary flash—I was the one who'd talked him into the senior center six years ago. "If it seems like you feel worse after going there, you may have to decide which is easier, going or not going."

"Yeah," he said dryly.

The cell phone crackled and died. Out in the country, the signal fading in and out, I texted: "Be over first thing tomorrow, to visit & take care of bills, love you."

"Okay," he texted back. It was 9:13 p.m., June 12.

The next day, I'd planned to go straight over, but first decided to call. When I got no answer, I got a bad, bad feeling. I called a friend, and something made me say, "I don't want to walk into that if he's done something." I'd verbalized my feeling; I already knew. I hung up and continued to call Dad, until my sister texted and we decided to meet there.

Dad was in bed, on his side, facing the doorway. He'd shot himself in the temple. My poor, sweet, old dad, may God have mercy on him for doing it and on me for being unable to forgive what led him to this point.

That evening, I sat on the couch with Rod, crying over what else I could've done.

"I should've done more. I loved him and should've tried harder. Maybe I could've prevented this," I sobbed.

As soon as I said it, suddenly, not two feet in front of me, came a very loud *SNAP, SNAP*—someone snapped their fingers in my face! It was a one-of-a-kind sound, recognizable and very loud in the quiet room, where moments before the only sound was my crying.

"Dad, is that you?!" I cried. I *knew* it was. "Please do it again if it was!" But the room was now still.

"Dad, ask God to forgive you. Call out for Him and watch for the light. Go toward the light. I love you, and I'm so very sorry," I said. The words had a strange echo. And I wondered if James could hear me too.

I knew it was Dad—and he was saying, "I'm here, snap out of it, you did all you could." I know he loved me, just by the fact that he came back. Maybe he regretted it and wanted to explain. Maybe his mind was clear now, and he could see what'd transpired. Maybe now he knew just what others did *to* him and *for* him. I felt no anger at Dad. Maybe I redirected it at myself. At least *I* was somebody I could beat up on—for losing my temper with her, for not being able to fix it, for not saying all the right things to cheer him up and make it better. In my family, I'd always been responsible for this "cheering up." If I hadn't been mired so deep in my own misery, maybe I *could've* prevented it. But I hadn't felt like being anyone's cheerleader. *I* needed someone to cheer *me* up now, and no one did. As I raged at myself for all my failings, I sank far deeper than the bottom of that familiar pit of despair. Now I was in the sub-basement of it.

We buried Dad right beside James. It was my birthday. Saying it was my worst one ever is an understatement. Now Mom, Dad, and James were together in the cold hard ground. And darkness pretty much ruled.

14

Tomorrow and Tomorrow and Tomorrow

I grieved for Dad quietly and turned further within. I knew the kind of despair Dad felt in those final moments. I'd been there myself. All I could think of was the body bag when they carried him out. I'd held back my tears until I saw it, sagging in the middle from his slight weight; he'd lost fifteen pounds by the end, from grief. A hazmat team, ludicrously dressed like spacemen to keep them safe from my eighty-year-old father's blood, was hired to do the cleanup—state regulations required it.

I moved his furniture and clothing out, trying not to see the splattered wall behind his bed. But somebody had to do this, and that somebody was me, as it'd always been. Cousin Joyce and her family helped me pack it all up. She's always been like a sister. I heard nothing from the companion—it was as though it'd never happened. The obituary made no mention of her, as it would've been ridiculous under the circumstances. Dad would've understood. After all that had transpired over the past six years, it was the only thing I *could* do.

I heard her family member was posting that "evil people were telling lies"—apparently me. When asked why Dad had done this, I'd simply been telling the true story of what transpired. His heart was broken.

That last time in the hospital, when Dad realized he had to move out, I'd sent an email recounting the relationship history to her family member—in case they didn't know the true story. I just wondered if they knew he'd been asked to leave so many times, and that each time, I had to find an apartment. I finally apologized in that email for losing my temper. I'd also stated it was probably best for both of them that he *did* leave this time, because obviously, this had been a pattern throughout the entire relationship. I'd even offered the hand of friendship, for Dad's sake, though it took all of my now-mangled "sociability." But after hearing myself called "evil," I vowed to jettison the *real* evil in my life. This whole situation was first on my list. No more time wasted on this particular "darkness." But it was too late for Dad.

Numb and in a fog, I focused on settling Dad's estate. I just wanted it to be over with. This time I was ready to move on. Unlike James, Dad's after-death message was very clear; with a snap of his fingers, he communicated that he still existed. I knew he came back to me because he understood how devastated I'd be. And I hoped he was on his way to Heaven, in spite of what's said about suicides. I believe God knows our hearts and when our minds aren't thinking straight. I know for sure Dad's wasn't. To do this as a lifelong Christian and a good and decent man, it couldn't have been. He was beaten down, systematically destroyed, piece by piece. But it was really almost unbelievable, on top of losing James.

———

Every week, Rod and I went to visit James's grave. We spent all week trying to pretend it hadn't happened, trying desperately to go on, going to work, dealing with everyday problems. But on that trip to the cemetery and back, we let it all come pouring out, no longer pretending for the rest of the world. It was *our* time; no one else could feel what we felt, and this is when we shared it.

"Will you drive?" Rod asked on our next trip.

Hmmm, that's weird, I thought. *He always drives.* I made a mental note of this new pattern. "Do you feel okay?" I responded.

"Yeah, I just don't want to drive right now," he answered.

"Okay," I shrugged, getting behind the wheel.

All the way out, we discussed James and the sentencing, wondering how long it'd be until she'd go to prison. We discussed Dad, and our terrible depression. When we got to the cemetery, we cried at James's graveside, talking to him, not caring if anyone could hear or what they might think of the two crazy people. We no longer cared about a lot of stuff.

We made it back to town, still talking about James's death, still consumed by it, both of us unsure we could go on like this. At the red light a block and a half from home, engrossed in the destruction of all my hopes and dreams for the future—James's wedding, becoming a grandmother, all the things that would never happen now—I suddenly felt my psychic tingle. I slowly came back to the present, acknowledging it, and looked up to see a small woman in the crosswalk, directly across the street from me.

"That looks like her," I whispered, half to myself.

"What?" asked Rod.

"That woman there," I repeated louder, nodding in her direction, "it looks like her." Staring intently at the figure making its way down the street, I brushed my hair back to see. I focused on her, trying to tell if it really *was* her. The light turned.

"I'm turning left. See if it's her," I said. She didn't know our car, and I didn't care if she did. I was totally focused and nothing else mattered. It was just getting dark and I couldn't quite tell.

"I don't know her," said Rod. "I only met her once, years ago." He glanced at me and I heard the concern in his voice. "What are you gonna do? Maybe we should just go home. This isn't helping any." The woman continued on down the street, oblivious.

But my focus was drawn to a single-minded purpose: look her in the face. All the pain, the depression, the outrage at what she'd done to us and to James, the rage over her tactics—everything—all coalesced into this one bright, white-hot urge to face her down.

She was enjoying life. *James would never enjoy life again.* I'd heard through James's friends (who worked with her) about her birthday plans (which was the day after James's), about her laughter at lighthearted moments throughout her day, acting as though she hadn't a care in the world. *James would never have another birthday. James would never laugh again.* There'd been ongoing vandalism at the small shrine erected by James's friends at the crash site. Then there was the rumor that James was drinking that day, and when it was traced directly to the restaurant where her son, James's old high school friend, worked, it was the last straw.

James had passed all the toxicology tests cleanly—the doctors told us he wouldn't have been considered for organ donation if he hadn't. The rumor was just another ploy by her "team" to disparage James, to lessen her culpability in his death. I wouldn't allow him to be smeared. He couldn't defend himself now. And she was a murderer. Of my only child.

"I just need to see if it's her," I said, turning around and heading back toward her again. As I went past this time, under the blue-white glare of the streetlight, I confirmed that it *was*.

"It's her," I whispered. And that was my last moment of coherent thought as my intellect was drowned by a seething, churning rage that boiled up from somewhere deep below even the sub-basement level. I felt homicidal. It felt great. I would face her and confront this monster for what she'd done to me, to us, to James. She'd single-handedly destroyed all our lives with her selfish party-animal ways.

"C'mon, let's go home. This is pointless," said Rod uneasily, looking at me.

But I was locked in, obsessed with it all, with the lack of justice, the ongoing torment from her behavior. I had no real thoughts, no plan, just the smoldering, never-ending pain buzzing in my head, the pain that had paralyzed my life. *This* was the source of all my misery, *this one small woman*. I hated her. I had to face this ultimate darkness, this devil incarnate.

I made a U-turn to go the direction she was walking, but I'd lost her. I knew where she lived, so I headed there, detached from myself, not recognizing anything except my swelling fury and the need to look her in the eye. As I turned into the alley beside her house, she suddenly stepped out from the yard she'd cut across, five feet in front of me.

"Stop, stop!" yelled Rod. "What are you doing? Let's go. Let's just go home."

I barely heard him. The sudden pounding of blood in my ears was surging like hot lava through a too small chute. I was in a zone I'd never been in before—unaware of anything but her, not thinking, acting only on impulse, my savagery bordering on madness and overpowering all reason.

With fifty feet to go to reach her back gate, she walked down the alley in my headlights.

Hands clenched on the wheel, I crept along behind her, and suddenly realized I could kill her. I could easily run her over, back up, and do it again and again. I could see it in my mind, all my revenge fantasies come true. I felt my rage overpower me—my left side tingling and warning me, my sight narrowed to that space five feet in front of my bumper where the monster who killed my baby, the love of my life, my light and my hope, now walked. There was no thought, no sound now but a high-pitched ringing in my ears, like the sound that comes before you pass out. There was only blackness all around and the woman in front of me. At a snail's pace, I followed, ready, mesmerized, more focused than I'd ever been in my life, and time stood still. Forty feet, thirty-five, thirty, twenty-five, twenty, she was almost home now. Rod screamed at me.

"Stop it!"

I barely heard him, but some little piece of humanity that still hung on within me—that light within us all—held me back a moment more, and suddenly James's face was in my mind's eye. And finally I heard him speak. "Mom, it's all good," he said.

The shock of being so suddenly yanked from the depths of my rage back up to the real world left me dizzy. Five feet away from her fence, I shook my head, dazed, and slowly pulled around beside her. She was on the passenger side, and I rolled down Rod's window.

"Who are you people? I don't even know you," she said as she turned to face us, uncertainty flickering across her face in the ambient light of a neighbor's porch.

"You killed our son," Rod said, his voice shaking. I stared raptly at her, at the black hollows of her eye sockets in shadow, mute with wordless, inexpressible hate, my tongue feeling thick in my mouth.

"No I didn't," was her infuriating answer.

My rage blossomed again, coming up fast at her shameless denial. I wanted to hurt her, to kill her, to exterminate the object responsible for my despair, the destroyer of my precious Jamie. The floodgates opened and up surged all the bile that had crushed me under its weight. I called her every evil name I ever knew, ruing the day she was born, and when I'd spent only a fragment of my rage, I suddenly came to again, realizing the rage was bottomless. There was no end to it and there never would be...and I was unable to control it...if it overtook me again, I might never come back.

Once again, this time willfully, picturing James's face to save me, I drove away. And once again, just as quickly as the rage ignited, it clicked off, leaving me breathless, sick, shaking, and horrified by how easy it would've been to kill her—knowing I almost did it, that I *wanted* to do it, and it would've given me pleasure. Numb with shock, bewildered and still detached, I asked Rod what had happened. "Who was that? That wasn't me. Who was that?"

For a while I expected the police to come get me—until I realized it's not illegal to tell someone what you think of them, as long as you don't threaten them. I couldn't believe this had happened, that it had seemed *set up* to happen. What were the odds? About the same as James's cars being systematically destroyed by drunks, about the same as her coming home drunk at the same millisecond James was there trying to avoid traffic on that side street. A few seconds either way and *none* of it would have happened. It felt like years in the making, like each predestined event lined up to cause the inevitable cascade of doom, all crashing down to this one very moment. It felt like I'd been set up to make the choice; I'd been given the chance to fully become the darkness.

So many times I'd stared it down—each time worse than the last: the haunted house, the violent boyfriend, the overdose, the illness, the companion, Dad's end, and finally my son's murderer. *I'll wish and pray it away*, I'd said as a child. *I will not deal with this*, I'd said as an adult. *I can make things good by the force of my will,* my lifelong denial insisted; *I'll banish this from my life.* But what you avoid, you attract, they say—if you gaze into the abyss, the abyss gazes into you; battle not with monsters lest ye become a monster. This time, I almost became the monster.

That night, I fell asleep missing James, afraid of myself now and what I knew I was capable of. That night, my sweet James woke me with the sound of his air-kisses in my room, a sound I'd longed for so often.

"Oh, James! This is the clearest you've been, sweetheart. This is what I needed more than anything!" I told him out loud.

Somehow I knew this was his way of telling me I chose the right path. I'd come full circle. I knew that James *was* the light now, and that the light is both *his* source and *mine.* I knew then I'd see him again when I died, as long as I stayed in that light. There's no question I want to stay in that light now. I hope I can…

––––––––

I've learned much since James's death: I know now that there is light and darkness in us all, and this darkness works overtime to influence us. But so does the light, in its own quiet way—the joy of past memories, the remembrance of the peace that comes from the love of a child, and the proof of that love in the sound of that deceased child's kiss. Somehow, I chose the light on that difficult day, and I have to believe I'll choose it again in the future when I'm inevitably tested—when she's free again. Dad chose the darker way. I pray for him a lot, as I do for James, and for myself.

I know it'll always be hard for me, always a struggle against the dark influence of the world, but it's a worthy struggle. I believe I must be diligent in holding it back, doing whatever I can, because "they" won't stop, and "they" are always allowed to set us up to fall. And sometimes that only becomes apparent in the fullness of time. I think I let it in, or made myself noticeable; whether from the Ouija or just by having or using psychic gifts. I won't know until the next life. I think the old witch saw it somehow, following me, and that's why she brought it up. But we ultimately choose our own direction. I think this is what the strange messenger was telling me that night thirty years ago at the nightclub. Maybe he was trying to warn me, maybe he wasn't evil, but good. Just as the bag lady, the "messenger" who encountered my little brother Dane, was good. It's the free-will thing again. Ultimately, you must choose your path.

I remember how proud James was of the psychic streak in his family, always wanting readings for his friends and asking for one himself the week before he died. I was in a hurry, so I read his palm and did a quick layout of his cards. Both showed what was about to

happen. I'm grateful I didn't understand what I was seeing, probably because it would've been unthinkable.

I interpreted what I saw as a huge change coming,
which fit with what was going on in his life. Now I think
that my interpretation wasn't too far wrong. The biggest
change we'll ever undergo is our transition to the after-
life. I just didn't realize it was James's time to make that
journey. And I'm glad I didn't see it. Maybe God in His
mercy holds back this gift at times like these.

But for now, I have a bit more peace. For now at least,
everything in the garage is just as James left it. His clothes
are scattered and draped over chairs, the ashtrays full of
butts, the notebooks full of lyrics, and skate parts everywhere, as if he just stepped out for a smoke. If he stops in,
he'll know; above all, I want him to feel secure—in death
as he did in life. And that we'll never forget him. He's the
wise one now; he knows what we here on earth do not—
he knows the mystery beyond. He knows love never dies,
and neither do we. And I know he'll be waiting for me
when it's my turn. I've let go of James as much as I ever
can, and I'm glad he hasn't entirely let me go. I feel he's at
peace. And his visits give me peace, and strength to go on.

I stay in the light now as much as possible, I stay close
to God. Closer than I've ever been, and it feels good. I've
learned that love is all that matters. James already knew this,
and he taught the rest of us in so many concrete ways. My
career, my obsession with musical self-perfection, nothing
means as much as James did. Nothing meant more to me

than that love for him. I'm so glad now that I spoiled him and made him my favorite project almost all the years of his life. So glad.

———————

The phone rings. I let the machine take it. It's my investigator friend, Brian, asking advice on a case. I go back to my writing, trying to finish this book before I call back. The phone rings again, and again the machine takes the message; it's a lady, wanting to schedule a reading party. I sigh and go back to writing. *Almost done…* They're really backing up now, the readings. How funny that every time I decide to back away from the psychic world, the requests come in twice as fast. *What you avoid you attract,* I think. The phone rings again a few minutes later; it's my old L.A. music publisher wanting to pitch my song to LeAnn Rimes. It's been years since we did business together. So the music biz keeps coming back around too, and that's okay. I won't be chasing any of it anymore; the old obsessions are gone now, gone with James. I don't care as much as I used to—it just doesn't matter. So again, what I avoid, I seem to attract.

Above all, I still want to help people, so I'll probably do that. I know God knows my heart, and that's what's most important. I also now know—and accept—that I may never get the answers I crave, that I may never understand: *Why me? Why this life? Why James? Why these abilities I never asked for?*

I look up from my writing and survey the quiet room. There's the floor register with a splash of gold paint, courtesy of two-year-old James upending the gallon; the oak pillars he climbed as a boy, hanging from the transom—our game—until I tickled him into dropping; the nearly invisible black thread he hung from the highest spindle on the stairs so his GI Joe could rappel to the floor; the grade-school picture on the desk beside the front door that his girlfriends invariably "awww'd" over while he laughed. I've left those things where they were all these years since he was little. I couldn't let them go then, and now it's even harder. The whole house is a monument to James in these ways. And maybe that little black GI Joe thread explains better than anything my love for him—holding on to the memories represented by this thread, and this one little thread, a metaphor for all that's left of his life.

Life moves on without James. A series of changes have come and gone since he died: a new bridge down the road, a new company in the old Laundromat across the street where skating practice occurred weekly, his old cat gone missing last May, his old dog fourteen years old and in her last days. Almost everything seems the same, but he's gone. At first, this bothered me. In so many ways, my world had ended. Yet things went on the same without him. The seasons changed, the world and we grew older. But he'll always be young and beautiful, and not quite twenty-five.

Soon his killer will be walking the streets, free again, her debt to society paid, while James is gone forever, at least physically. I wait for the "test" of seeing her again, the next "setup" I'm led into. Her sentence was eighteen months; but mine is life. It's so hard not to get to see what James would've become, not to see him married, never becoming a dad. Knowing I'll never be a grandma, that really gets to me. It's hard to ever be normal again, at least the "normal" I'd become accustomed to. I veer my mind away from these thoughts, and focus on peace. I mustn't let them take me over again. *It's so quiet here now. It's still so hard.* "James, I miss you," I say to the quiet room, suddenly feeling something, feeling him there maybe.

All at once, from the corner where it's been propped since he died, I hear my first guitar—a gift at my sweet-sixteen party—play a single note. James loved that guitar and took it on his travels, always followed by my warning to "be careful with that; it'll be yours someday, but for now, I'd hate to see it broken." It's never played like this before, not in all the time it's been there. I get a sudden rush of emotion and hope—

"James, is that you?"

Epilogue

We planned the annual James Short Memorial Session that first August after James died. It was a good distraction for me and his friends. A festival and skating session with proceeds going to charity held at the local skate park, James's favorite hangout. James's best friend, a pro skater, arrived from California beforehand. I was exhausted, so I turned in early while he and Rod stayed up talking. They'd been discussing coming to terms with James's death.

"This whole house is full of James's things. But it seems strange that all that's left is this handful of trinkets while he's gone." The moment Rod said this, the TV shut off. James's friend sat open-mouthed. Rod nodded knowingly. Both the cable box and the power were shut off. They knew it was James. "What the heck, James, is that you?" James's friend asked. As soon as the words left his mouth, the TV switched back on! This seemed pretty definitive. James's friend was convinced that James wanted him to know he was here, and still his best friend.

The next night at the skate park, I stood in the middle of the food tent. I'd set up the tables and was deep in thought on what was needed for the next day's event.

Overwhelmed by twenty things to do, I got a strange feeling and looked up. Headed toward me was a small group, a dark-haired older man leading the way, smiling. My heart skipped a beat as I watched him cross the dusty lot, and suddenly I knew; this man was carrying my son's heart deep within him.

He stuck out his hand and introduced himself. My eyes filled when he touched my hand.

"I'm so glad you came," I told him. "I hope it wasn't too much for you."

"It's all good," he said—and I knew then that James was part of him.

He'd driven from Massachusetts and had been through quite an ordeal, hooked up to a machine for six months while waiting for a heart. He insisted on manning the grill all day. James's friends asked if they could put their hands on his chest, to feel James's heart. We could see he was reserved, but also very kind. He understood the depth of what had happened to us and was gracious, grateful for James's ultimate gift.

It must've been difficult for them to imagine facing us—after all, they were celebrating their father's life being saved by James's death—but I let them know it was the one bright light in the darkness of that time. The other recipients I've spoken with, each deeply grateful for James's gift of life, have a standing invitation to the JSMS. James would've been proud. The session has thrown us a lifeline, as James's ultimate gift threw them a lifeline.

———

My old friend Sarah called one night, in a panic, crying and scared out of her wits. Apparently, on a lark, she'd had a ghost hunter come to her house. She'd been hearing noises and thought maybe Evan was trying to reach her. The investigator asked some questions, using a digital voice recorder.

"When he played it back, the first thing we heard was a deep voice saying "*stop it!*" she cried. "Then something growling and spitting. I'm too terrified to even be in my house, please help me!"

"What else did it say?" I asked her, well aware that most spirits don't growl or spit.

"Oh God, it said my name, then "*you're dead now.*" Sarah was beside herself with fear. I didn't blame her. She innocently thought they'd have a fun night imitating the popular paranormal shows, and it turned into sheer horror at what existed, invisible, in her personal space. Once you hear something like that, you can't un-hear it. I told her I couldn't be sure, but I suspected this was something other than just a ghost, due to the threats and growling. I honestly didn't want anything to do with it. I'd faced this "darkness" enough.

"Have you used a Ouija board?" I asked her.

"Yes, we didn't think anything of it. We used it a lot."

I knew this was what could open the door and, unless you were well versed in protecting yourself, allow entities in.

I told her she'd have to make a concerted effort to get rid of this. I didn't know if she really understood that part. She said she went to a preacher to have him pray for her, and she couldn't concentrate on his prayer, which seemed strange to her. *That is not a good sign,* I thought.

"Sarah, you'll be okay, but you should do a few things to keep yourself safe. First, remember, God's in charge, and any demonic entities are scared of Him." I told her to say the St. Michael prayer, which is good protection against demonic infestations. Holy water and prayers spoken aloud in the house are among the things that can be used to break this type of an infestation. The problem is knowing whether it's in the house or around her. When I was there four years earlier for her party, I hadn't felt anything like this. I thought she'd probably let it in since. Maybe it had even had something to do with Evan's death. I hoped not.

However, I knew it was up to her to change her ways somewhat, and leave no room for it in her life. I hoped she was scared enough to do that.

That night Sarah sent me a picture she took of some kids at her house, and behind them, in the door, were three ghostly faces peering in. She sent a picture her young son had drawn, a frightening-looking "thing" peeking around a doorframe with hollow black eyes and a black slash of a mouth. It looked just like the face in the first picture. This worried me for his sake.

"Only you can take control of this," I told her. "Do it, for your son's sake."

Sarah took my advice seriously, began taking her boy to church, and followed my directions. She also changed the negatives in her life. The incidents lightened up dramatically. And Sarah has a newfound respect for the things that exist just beyond our ability to see.

I hoped this wasn't the same evil that had followed me. I hoped I didn't bring it with me all those years ago when I did the reading party at her house. If she needs my help again, I'll help her if I can, but I'm very cautious now, and make it a priority to protect myself and those around me, at least those still left. It's not a game as so many think. There are so few answers and so many questions. And I've questioned every single thing I once thought I knew for sure.

———

As I've struggled to relive the events of James's life and death for this book, I put off writing about his end as long as I could. I wrote the chapters before it and right up to it, then the aftermath, still putting off the inevitable. The day finally came that I was nearly done, except for the chapter about James's death. So I began to write.

I read it aloud to Rod to get his take on each scene. We both cried—it truly brought it all back, even things we'd forgotten. I read the story of arriving at the scene, the helicopter, the hospital. *James never knew what happened to him,* I thought. *I wonder if he can hear me.* I finished and dried my eyes; I'd had all I could stand for one night. It was a slow process writing one little piece at a time like this, but it was the best I could do.

I headed straight up to bed, and I lay there, heart aching, saying prayers for James.

"I love you, James," I whispered, and instantly a loud thump came from the hallway, which shook the small tables and rattled the lamps.

"Was that you?" Rod called from the bathroom.

"No," I yelled back, "but I just told James, out loud, that I loved him!"

"It came from right here in the hall!" Rod said, sticking his head in the door.

I lay there and thought about the fact that I'd just read out loud, from his parents' perspective, what James's end had been like. I felt hope that maybe he was letting me know he'd heard. Rod stuck his head in again a few seconds later.

"I just heard that electric crackling sound start up, right beside me," he said. "The same sound I heard in the studio the night James died."

I knew that on the bathroom shelf, right beside where Rod was standing, I kept James's watch with the crystal cracked from being hit, as well as the locks of hair he'd trimmed the day before—all wrapped up with the Kleenex that I'd wiped his chapped lips with in the hospital. Another batch of things I just couldn't let go of yet. The crackling sounds came from very near those little leftover pieces of James. I'm convinced these unusual things that happen are his way of staying in touch with us.

———

James continues to make his presence known in so many big and little ways. We'd left the light on in the garage since James died. Our electric bills were sky high, but it didn't matter. In case he stopped in there, he'd know—I left the light on for him. Also since he'd died, we'd made sure that any changes around the house and in our lives came in small increments. Every time I started to throw something away—even small items like an empty bottle of shampoo or a bottle of ketchup—I'd think "James touched this," or "this was here when James was here." I knew this was crazy, but I honored it anyway, not knowing how else to deal with it. I laughed at myself. *Soon I'll be one of those poor hoarders like on that TV show.* So change came slowly, and the big changes, I told myself, someday maybe, but not yet.

Not long ago, on the way home from a gig, I noticed the light in the garage had finally burned out. We decided maybe it was time to let it go. This was a pretty big change for us. The following weekend, James's old skater friend Gary from Detroit called to see if he could stay on their way through the area. That night we sat telling "James" stories. When I went into the kitchen, I saw the old familiar light on in the garage. It'd been off for weeks. It took the decision out of our hands. It was back on again. We don't know how. But it's still on.

————

Finally, I'd like to say that I believe we're all weighed and measured every day—the cracks in our armor assessed, the strengths and weaknesses noted. Where is this person able to be tempted, where is that person able to be tricked into working for the "other side"; through pride, vanity, anger, or greed.

It's not for me to judge anyone, nor you. We need to look inside ourselves every day and ask—at any given moment, at major or minor decisions—which "side" am I working for? Which "side" does this benefit most? Sounds paranoid, I know, but now I believe it wholeheartedly. We're so wrapped up in our world, the here and now, we forget our mission.

I still struggle every day with how to use psychic gifts, weighing where best to use them, or whether to use them at all. I think it'll always be this way for me. But God knows my heart, and that gives me hope that everything will be okay now. I have to trust this, it's all I've got.

In my own way, I'm trying to give back, to do things that help others. I focus on the Memorial Session, the JSMS as we call it. This helps me heal, it makes me feel like something good came out of something so very bad. We finally released James's songs in a double CD titled *Tread Water*. I recently signed them to my L.A. music publisher, "Rex Benson Music/Pen Music Group" along with one of my own. And then I got the call that James's song "On the Prowl" was placed in the Matthew McConaughey red band movie trailer of *Killer Joe*. I'm excited about this—I know James would be too. His legacy of music lives on, so in turn, *he* lives on.

I try to focus on the good things left to me. I just can't dwell on the bad. There's too much of it; you sort of have to let it go. What I've mostly learned over all the years is that you can't reason with crazy, and you can't argue innocent intent to someone's evil certainty. When Mom was in the deepest throes of dementia, she sometimes dreamed things and then thought they'd really happened. I would gently try to explain how the doctors said her mind might play tricks on her once in a while. She'd become quite irritated at this, offended by remarks that, to her, seemed completely ridiculous.

"There's nothing wrong with my mind!" she'd indignantly reply, insulted. After a few times, I decided just to let the delusions go by without comment. It spared her the reality of her craziness. She deserved that much.

And with evil intent, you just can't shed love and light and positive outlook on someone who believes the worst. It's impossible to change those beliefs, or at least, it's not my job. Evil doesn't see evilness in itself. Crazy doesn't see craziness in itself. So save yourself some trouble trying to change this. "Let God sort 'em out," as the punch line to an old joke we used to tell goes.

Our focus will lie with whatever we most love or hate in this life. James and Dad both loved relationships most and were the better for it, though Dad's life ended badly. Even so, love is all that really matters, and I can't fault Dad for loving, only for not loving more discerningly. God knows we're all guilty of that at times, I certainly have been.

I know there may be forces against this story getting out. Though it's true, it does damage by illuminating certain things that thrive best in the dark. I'm tired of pretending that everything's okay, so I'll spread this book, my little bit of light, my little bit of truth, everywhere I can. Maybe I told too much, maybe I didn't tell enough—but it is what it is now.

I'm almost done, so we'll see what happens next. My dream of me, Dad, and James going on that long trip has come two-thirds true. I'm waiting to see where the next adventure takes me. I wear a small gold teardrop pendant—a bit of James's ashes are inside—so he goes with me everywhere now. I live for him; he loved life so much. He loved laughter and light. In the end, all I'm really sure of is which side I want to be on. Which side do *you* want to be on? If it's the same one as me, I want to convey the only important thing to all of you reading this: Stay in the light…

————

It is very beautiful over there.
  Thomas A. Edison's words while nearing death.

Psychic Chitchat –
Whys, Hows, and My Two Cents

Over the years, I've come to the conclusion that this psychic gift isn't evil, as some religious people teach. Throughout Christianity there are examples of psychic abilities being used, and most are found in the Bible. Prophecy or clairvoyance, precognition, and prophetic dreams are all represented. I personally have a strong belief in good and evil forces. I've witnessed them first hand, and I want to always be aligned with the good, and that's reflected in my methods.

I've always been asked, "How do you do this?" According to the religion I was raised in, I say a prayer and ask to be shown whatever the person needs to know. I cover my eyes and wait for pictures to form. At first it's only darkness, then light begins to come from all directions and forms pictures, words, or phrases. When I was young, I thought everybody could do this. And I think I was right, to some extent. Although a few people I experimented with couldn't do anything, most people had some ability. Of course, there's definitely a learning curve involved, but I believe it's possible to teach others to be open enough. It seems those who want it most, get it.

I've come to recognize the meanings of certain symbols that the light "composes." For instance, a cross usually means someone's passed away or soon will. A heart means that a relationship is the issue, as does a diamond ring. A street name may be spelled out, or the name of someone important or some personal item will be formed. At other times, I hear names or information, almost as though it's whispered to me in my head, which is known as clairaudience in technical psychic terms. It does take a lifetime though, to make sense of it all. And I'm still learning.

Even now, every time I'm asked to "see" something for somebody, I get a flash of fear and self-doubt ("What if it doesn't work this time?") because I can't force it to work—it functions independently of my will. Sometimes it's stronger, at other times weaker. But it usually does work. Every time something startling is revealed for the people I'm reading, the look on their faces lets me know they're no longer skeptical.

Not only does this psychic streak run in my family, but so does some insanity in the generation of my great-grandmother; it's trickled down in greater or lesser degrees. A couple of Great-Grandma's siblings were institutionalized, and it apparently was so hush-hush no one spoke of it. Or at least, it wasn't passed down to our generation. There also seemed to be a touch of religious fanaticism, but that's not to say these relatives weren't decent, hard-working citizens as well.

Science points to a connection between psychic abilities and schizophrenia. Many psychic people have a family history of psychosis—a genetic predisposition that some believe is statistically significant. In layman's terms, it goes something like this: you are "open" to either abilities or psychosis, due to loosened boundaries. The good news is they also claim it runs hand in hand with high intelligence and creativity. When you're open a little too far, any or all of these are possible. Luckily, I never had to deal with major mental illness, but it was rough for a while when I was young and trying to figure out just what was going on.

If you're born with any psychic gifts, periods of soul-searching are inevitable. When those gifts are complicated by a strict upbringing, as mine were, the search for answers can be terrifying. Movies like *The Exorcist* and *The Omen* had me checking my hairline for the 666 birthmark or convinced that I was possessed. What else could explain sensing things, knowing things no one else knew, saw, or felt? Early on, I wondered if I was crazy, but after the premonitions and "knowings" had been corroborated and confirmed a few times, I knew I wasn't.

Those who are good at self-promotion often do well as psychics, though I'm not much of a fan of this myself.

A great example of good psychic self-promotion happened in my area a few years ago. There'd been a missing person case, and because of the circumstances, it was all over the local headlines and had everyone in an uproar. A police officer's nine-months-pregnant girlfriend was missing from her home, which showed signs of a struggle. Her two-year-old son by the same officer was found wandering in the house alone.

I was driving as I listened to a radio interview of a famous local "psychic." She was expounding on what had happened to the woman, saying she saw lots of blood, and she and the DJs were all inferring the unborn baby had been cut out of the woman and stolen, as had been happening around the country. Something just didn't feel right, so as I sat at a stoplight, I closed my eyes and asked to be shown what had happened.

Immediately, I saw pictures form: a diamond ring, a fist coming down, and an "*X*" marking the spot which I'd come to recognize as something buried. I instantly knew that her police officer boyfriend had done it and that there was some kind of relationship violence. The ring signified a relationship. The *X* means something buried; I assumed this meant her, unfortunately. I listened to the psychic go on about all the blood and I knew she wasn't seeing what happened. I immediately emailed the station about what I'd seen, but it would've been hard to retract what the psychic had said to the tens of thousands of listeners. And it would've been hard to naysay the "famous" psychic. So my message went nowhere.

Later, when it was released that her two-year-old son told the police, "Mommy's crying. Mommy broke the table. Mommy's in the rug," and, later, "Daddy's mad," everyone knew who'd done it. Then they found the woman in a shallow grave, and the officer was eventually convicted. Was this another case of a fake psychic who somehow built up a lot of media exposure through self-promotion, or was it just that she didn't see anything at that moment so she had to make something up? No psychic is right 100 percent of the time, but the honest thing to do is to say you can't see anything. That's the way real psychic abilities act. It shows your humanity and dispels the "TV psychic" image.

Mine is not a popular approach. And to be fair, maybe these psychics just want to be everything to everybody. The reason this is so disturbing is because people come to a psychic needing help, advice, guidance, and understanding. As in any profession, charlatans exist, but it's a bit worse in the psychic world because it's sometimes easier to fake, and more is at stake. I wouldn't want to be in the charlatans' shoes though—I wouldn't want their karma! I also believe that if a psychic, or anyone for that matter, isn't humble about their gifts, they seem to eventually be smacked down by God, karma, the universe, or whatever deity or force of nature you happen to believe in.

In my personal opinion, I believe people could get the same answers a psychic gets by asking God themselves, but they have no confidence in their ability to hear Him. And finally, I believe that demonic forces need to be dealt with by professionals—people in the church. Laypersons risk great personal harm by trying to exorcise a demon. I don't recommend trying it if you value your health, sanity, or even the lives of those close to you. Paranormal shows have made this hidden realm popular lately. "Ghost hunters" are charging to remove spirits in homes, but the truth is, no one can guarantee this. Like the people they once were, they'll leave only if they *want* to. Beware of unethical practitioners. In any new or popular movement, schemers will always find ways to fleece people.

———

I spent my whole life disavowing my experiences, running from spirits and hauntings, and so, in essence, running from myself, until finally I had no choice but to embrace it. Lately, I've had to embrace all of life, the good and the bad. Some things I brought upon myself, but in many, I was an innocent victim, though I've tried to avoid that victim mentality. I've always tried to shake it off, put a smile on my face, and carry on. This has been harder to do since James died, and in a way, this book is me "shaking it off."

To those of you who are just beginning your own psychic journey, whether as a seeker of knowledge or a possessor of abilities, I wish you peace. Use the knowledge or the powers for the greater good. And most of all, don't fear the gifts or believe others who tell you they're entirely evil. There is so much more to it than that. They are, above all, special, even though they carry a heavy burden at times. I believe they are a gift from God, and we must use them to benefit our fellow man however we can. I wish you the best in your journey to understand the nature of *your* gifts. We're all seekers, and on the same journey.

———

Prayer for safety in any haunted house or haunted workplace:

> *Saint Michael the Archangel, defend us in battle, be our protection against the wickedness and snares of the devil. May God rebuke him we humbly pray; and do thou, O Prince of the Heavenly Host, by the power of God, thrust into hell Satan and all evil spirits who wander throughout the world seeking the ruination of souls. Amen.*

Never Say Goodbye
A Medium's Stories of Connecting with Your Loved Ones
PATRICK MATHEWS

"I'm a normal guy … I just speak to dead people."

When he was six years old, Patrick Mathews came face to face with the spirit of his dead Uncle Edward. As an adult, Mathews serves as a vessel of hope for those who wish to communicate with their loved ones in spirit.

The stories Mathews tells of his life and the people he has helped are humorous, heartwarming, and compelling. Part of his gift is in showing the living that they can still recognize and continue on-going relationships with the departed.

Mathews takes the reader on a roller coaster of emotional stories, from the dead husband who stood by his wife's side during her wedding to a new man, to the brazen spirit who flashed her chest to get her point across. You will also learn step-by-step methods for recognizing your own communications from beyond.

978-0-7387-0353-4, 216 pp., 6 x 9   **$15.95**

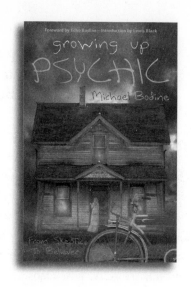

Foreword by Echo Bodine · Introduction by Lewis Black

growing up

PSYCHIC

Michael Bodine

From Skeptic
To Believer

Growing Up Psychic
From Skeptic to Believer
MICHAEL BODINE

What's it like to grow up psychic—in a family of psychics?

Michael Bodine was only seven when his family made a shocking discovery: he, his mother, and his siblings—including his sister, the renowned Echo Bodine—are psychic. What was it like to grow up in a house teeming with ghosts and psychic experimentation, contend with a mind-reading mother, befriend a spirit boy, and hunt ghosts with his sister Echo? And what happens when Michael's psychic talents become more of a burden than a blessing?

From adolescence to adulthood, this gripping memoir chronicles the wondrous, hair-raising, hilarious, and moving moments in Michael Bodine's life, punctuated by an ongoing struggle to come to terms with the paranormal. Discover how he rebounds from drug and alcohol dependency and learns to accept—and embrace—his unusual gifts.

978-0-7387-1961-0, 312 pp., 6 x 9   **$16.95**

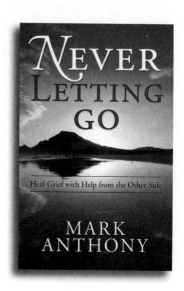

NEVER LETTING GO

Heal Grief with Help from the Other Side

MARK ANTHONY

Never Letting Go
Heal Grief with Help from the Other Side
MARK ANTHONY

After his mother's death, Mark Anthony was devastated—until he experienced the impossible: a visit from her. This profound and life-changing experience not only helped him cope with crushing grief but inspired him to develop his gift of spirit communication and bring healing to others.

Opening up to the notion that life transcends death is the first powerful lesson in this engaging and uplifting guide to healing from grief. Evidence of the soul's immortality is illustrated in moving accounts of the author delivering life-affirming messages of forgiveness, gratitude, hope, and comfort from loved ones on the Other Side. By sharing his experiences and wisdom as a psychic lawyer and medium, Mark Anthony reveals the healing nature of spirit communication and the rewards of opening our hearts to beloved friends and family in spirit.

978-0-7387-2721-9, 288 pp., 5³⁄₁₆ x 8   **$15.95**

ANNIE WILDER

THE
TRUE
STORY
OF A
HAUNTED
HOUSE

HOUSE
of
SPIRITS
AND
WHISPERS

House of Spirits and Whispers
The True Story of a Haunted House
ANNIE WILDER

Annie Wilder suspected the funky 100-year-old house was haunted when she saw it for the first time. But nothing could have prepared her for the mischievous and downright scary antics that take place once she, her two children, and her cats move into the rundown Victorian home. Disembodied conversation, pounding walls, glowing orbs, and mysterious whispers soon escalate into full-fledged ghostly visits—provoking sheer terror that, over time, transforms into curiosity. Determined to make peace with her spirit guests, she invites renowned clairvoyant Echo Bodine over and learns fascinating details about each of the entities residing there.

Wilder's gripping tale provides a compelling glimpse into the otherworldly nature of the lonely spirits, protective forces, phantom pets, and departed loved ones that occupy her remarkable home.

978-0-7387-0777-8, 192 pp., 6 x 9   **$14.99**

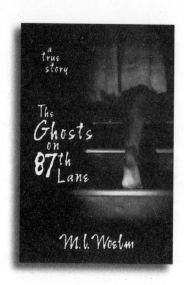

The Ghosts on 87th Lane
A True Story
M. L. WOELM

After moving her young family into their first house—a small suburban home in the Midwest—a series of strange and chilling events take place: unexplained noises, objects disappearing, lights going out by themselves, phantom footsteps. And then M. L. Woelm's neighbor confirms the horrifying truth: her house is haunted.

Beginning in 1968 and spanning three decades, this moving memoir chronicles the hair-raising episodes that nearly drove an ordinary housewife and mother to the breaking point. With friends who thought she was crazy and a skeptical, unsupportive husband who worked nights, the author was left all alone in her terror. How did she cope with disembodied sobs, eerie feelings of being watched, mysterious scratches appearing on her throat, and a phantom child's voice crying "Mommy!" in her ear?

978-0-7387-1031-0, 288 pp., 6 x 9   **$12.95**

Haunting Experiences
Encounters with the Otherworldly
Michelle Belanger

Working the graveyard shift at a haunted hotel, encountering a Voodoo spirit in New Orleans, helping the victim of an astral vampire attack... the supernatural has played a part in Michelle Belanger's life since the age of three. Yet she refuses to take the "unexplained" for granted, especially when the dead speak to her.

From haunted violins to dark fey, Belanger relives her thrilling experiences with haunted people, places, and things. Inspired to understand the shadowy truths about these paranormal mysteries, she examines each otherworldly encounter with a skeptical eye. What remains is a solid survey of the paranormal from a credible narrator, who also learns to accept her own gifts for spirit communication.

978-0-7387-1437-0, 264 pp., 6 x 9   **$15.95**